BLADE SLAP

A YEAR WITH THE RAF CHINOOK DISPLAY TEAM

Tom Mercer

AMBERLEY

First published 2019

Amberley Publishing
The Hill, Stroud
Gloucestershire, GL5 4EP

www.amberley-books.com

Copyright © Tom Mercer, 2019

The right of Tom Mercer to be identified as the Author of this work has been asserted in accordance with the Copyrights, Designs and Patents Act 1988.

ISBN 978 1 4456 8929 6 (paperback)
ISBN 978 1 4456 8930 2 (ebook)

British Library Cataloguing in Publication Data.
A catalogue record for this book is available from the British Library.

Typeset in 11pt on 13pt Sabon LT Std.
Typesetting by Amberley Publishing.
Printed in the UK.

CONTENTS

ACKNOWLEDGEMENTS

Writing a book has been an eye-opening experience and one that was much more difficult than I anticipated at times. The opportunity to put this book together was only made possible thanks to the brilliant team at RAF Odiham, who very early on recognised that there was a fantastic story to tell about life behind the scenes of a front-line display team.

Andy Donovan was the driving force behind getting my idea up and running at RAF Odiham and throughout the year he continued to keep on top of everything that was required from an official capacity to make sure that this book went to print. This wasn't the first time that Andy and I had worked together on something and I hope it won't be the last! Without Andy's perseverance, this book would likely have never seen the light of day. As much as I hate to admit it, he's also a superb photographer in his own right!

Along with Andy, Stuart Kynaston, Vince Bartlett, Gav Anderson, Matt Smyth, James Kennedy, Dave Cawood and Olley Leaming also deserve a special mention. These guys made my photography a dream and allowed me to experience and capture scenes that had never been seen before. I have never worked with a group of people that have relaxed in front of the camera so quickly; within a couple of weeks I could pretty much fade into the background and let them get on with their jobs, and that ultimately led to some of the most natural photography I've ever produced. Thank you for being so open and welcoming throughout the year. It was a pleasure to see you grow together as a team and be part of such a special year in the RAF. Thank you to Chris Warr as well for building my project into the Station's media plan for the year. Without this, I wouldn't have been able to capture half of the content that's buried within these pages.

While we are talking about the team, I'd like to extend a thank you to not only their families and friends that continue to support them throughout their careers, but also to each and every one of you that followed the team throughout the 2018 display season. Friends and family are everything, and air shows and display teams wouldn't exist without the enthusiast community.

Thank you to Group Captain Lee Turner, Station Commander RAF Odiham, and Wing Commander John Eastlake, who had the sign-off on whether my project got off the ground (no pun intended) or not. Thanks to the permissions granted by both, I have been able to capture scenes, moments and anecdotes that will likely never be seen publicly again.

Thank you to the Ministry of Defence and Joint Helicopter Command for approving this book for public release.

Finally, a very special thank you to my fiancée, Charli, who has supported me every step of the way with this project. She put up with me being out and about at all hours of the day chasing this story, editing photos and writing the content of this book. Your encouragement helped massively when at times it didn't seem that everything was going the way it should have been. Thank you!

FOREWORD

The Royal Air Force has a proud tradition of Display Flying as part of its enduring focus on professionalism and excellence. The Chinook Display Team follows in this tradition and the display season of 2018 provided an opportunity to show the very best of the Chinook aircraft and those who operate it within the unique context of the Royal Air Force's centenary year. The 100th anniversary of the Royal Air Force, celebrated under the banner of RAF100 and the three themes of Commemorate, Celebrate and Inspire, set the scene for an extraordinary year and the small part the Chinook Display Team played in this has been wonderfully captured in the pages of this book. The Display Team itself of course is not just the aircrew, although their flying skill and professionalism is undeniable, it is also the engineers and support personnel without whom simply getting airborne would be unachievable. This is the story of their remarkable efforts and success during a challenging but hugely rewarding year.

Group Captain L. Turner BEng(Hons) RAF, Station Commander, Royal Air Force Odiham

INTRODUCTION

By trade I work in IT, a far cry from anything to do with aviation or photography, so how exactly did I get to be in a position where I could spend a whole year shadowing a Royal Air Force Display Team?

I was born and raised in Hook, a small village less than three miles from RAF Odiham in Hampshire. No matter where you are in the surrounding areas, you can almost always guarantee that at some point in the day you'll hear that infamous 'blade slap' sound of the Chinook helicopter. Growing up such a short distance from Odiham meant that I could not only hear them on a daily basis, but also see them flying overhead to and from the base. My family has no background in the military, nor in aviation; Odiham is solely responsible for my love of anything to do with flying.

The photographic side came to me much later in life. I studied Fine Art Photography as an A-Level at college, where I learnt how shots should be composed, how to control the exposure of an image and, more importantly, how to develop and process that exposure into a final piece. The first year was spent playing around with traditional photographic mediums to get a grasp for the basics: making your own pin hole cameras, shooting with both black and white and colour film, and even processing imagery in a proper dark room. It wasn't until the second year that we were even allowed to touch anything digital.

The course taught me everything I needed to know to get started with photography and I passed with flying colours. It wasn't until I started shooting outside of the curriculum that I realised how much we'd been limited in what we could achieve.

I started shooting aviation, like many others, at the numerous air shows that are held up and down the country. To begin with it was only a couple of shows a year but the more I photographed, the more I attended and by 2013 I was attending shows pretty much every other weekend throughout the summer.

2013 was a big year for me as it was the first time I had written anything substantial to accompany my photography. Having seen the Chinook display at a show the previous summer, I decided to write to the team at RAF Odiham to see if there was any chance of speaking to the team to get some words to go with the images on my blog. Amazingly, the team was interested and after attending a media day on base for the upcoming display season, the base asked if they could publish my article in the Station magazine; I couldn't believe it!

This was the first of many articles that I would end up producing in partnership with RAF Odiham, and over the course of a few years I started building some strong relationships and got the inside track on a lot of activity on base, most of which resulted in exclusive articles and interviews.

Fast forward to the end of 2017, when I was having a catch-up with Flt Lt Andy Donovan. I've got to know Andy quite well over the years and I've been fortunate enough to work with him on multiple occasions at Odiham. As a result, he let me know that he 'might' be selected for the 2018 Display Team and if so, would I be interested in writing an article on the team before the season got underway later in the year.

Of course, I said yes straight away without even thinking about it but the more we got chatting about plans for the upcoming season, the more I thought about what else I could potentially do. Having sat on my idea for a couple of days, I spoke to Andy again and tried to describe what I had in mind for the 2018 display season.

Back in 2013, following the initial interview at Odiham, I had been fortunate enough to go behind the scenes with the team at the Royal International Air Tattoo and capture some rarely seen insights into an air show weekend. My proposal for 2018 was to do something similar but to do it across the entire year, capturing everything from the very first display work-ups, right up to the final show at the end of the season. Projects like this have been carried out with the Red Arrows by numerous photographers and journalists but it had never been done with the Chinook Display Team.

The good news was that the team liked the idea and the guys were keen to understand a little more about what I wanted, what the content would be used for and what they could possibly do to make it happen.

On a cold January morning, we met up for a coffee and I took the guys through a series of imagery that I'd captured over the last few years to demonstrate the sort of scenarios I wished to capture. Spread out over the table between our coffees and my iPad were a few aviation photography books from legends such as Jamie Hunter, Richard Baker and Katsuhiko Tokunaga. We flicked through the pages together, discussing different ideas and talking about the sort of material that we could potentially get out of the display season. Due to the RAF's centenary, 2018 was set to be one of the busiest display seasons ever for the team and this meant that there would likely be some awesome opportunities along the way. Everyone around the table was happy but ultimately none of the team had the power to make it happen and sign it off. For anything to happen, the plans needed to be scrutinised and approved by the RAF Odiham Station Commander.

A couple of weeks passed, and I was all but ready to give up hope on my project. My phone buzzed in my pocket one afternoon and I had a message from Andy. I couldn't quite believe it: I was ready to open that message and accept defeat, but it had all gone to plan; the work had been approved and the display work-up was already in motion.

'Station Commander is happy. We've got the greenlight, you're going to have a very busy year!'

I shadowed the team right from the very beginning of their display work-ups. I was fortunate enough to sit in on briefings and internal meetings to really get a feel for what goes on behind closed doors. It really was a case of being a fly on the wall, and having experienced nearly all of the challenges in person throughout 2018, I have a new-found respect for what those in the Royal Air Force are up against on a daily basis.

2018 was a year of firsts for me and I had a truly unbelievable experience working alongside the team. Getting to know each and every one of the team was an honour and it's a year that I'll treasure for the rest of my life.

Blade Slap is the story of the 2018 Royal Air Force Chinook Display Team and collates more than six months of photographic work.

Please join us as we bring you unprecedented access and take you on a journey behind the scenes of the RAF's only fully operational display team.

Enjoy the ride!

Tom Mercer

1

THE 2018 RAF CHINOOK DISPLAY TEAM

Display Captain – Flt Lt Stuart Kynaston

Stu grew up near Shrewsbury, where he lived until he left for university in 2004. In 2003 he was selected for a Sixth Form Scholarship to join the Royal Air Force as a pilot and upon completion of his A-Levels he elected to upgrade this to a University Bursary and study for a Mathematics degree. He graduated from the University of Bath in 2007, having been a member of Bristol University Air Squadron throughout his time as a student.

After completing Initial Officer Training at RAF College Cranwell in 2008, Stu then spent the next three years on various flying training courses, including eighteen months back in Shropshire, training at RAF Shawbury. After arriving at RAF Odiham to join the Chinook Force he reached the end of his Operational Conversion course in November 2011 and was posted to No. 27 Squadron. He has completed four operational tours in Afghanistan and numerous training exercises around the

Flt Lt Stuart Kynaston.

world. Stu has over 1,250 hours flying the Chinook, now flying as a Training Captain and an Instrument Rating Examiner, and has operated in temperate, maritime and desert environments.

Outside of work, Stu competes in long-distance triathlon, running and cycling events, as well as playing the piano and walking the dog.

Co-Pilot – Flt Lt Matt Smyth

Schmitty grew up with a military background, having had both of his parents serve in the Royal Air Force. He went to school in Stafford, where he grew up and joined the RAF in January 2007, after finishing his A-Levels. Following completion of Initial Officer Training at the Royal Air Force College Cranwell, he commenced flying training at RAF Church Fenton and later RAF Shawbury.

After graduating from his rotary-wing training in August 2010 Schmitty was posted to RAF Odiham and onto the Chinook Force, finishing the Operational Conversion Flight in November 2011 and moving to No. 27 Squadron. Flt Lt Smyth has over 1,300 flying hours and has deployed four times to Afghanistan. He has taken part in multiple training exercises throughout Europe and America, as well as a detachment to the Falkland Islands in the South Atlantic. He is a qualified Training Captain and currently serves as No. 27 Squadron's Deputy Training Officer, responsible for the programming of squadron sorties.

Matt enjoys various outdoor pursuits, such as mountaineering, adventure sports and skiing.

Flt Lt Matt Smyth.

Co-Pilot – Flt Lt Andy Donovan

Andy grew up in Oxfordshire and attended King Alfred's Academy in Wantage before gaining a BSc (Hons) degree in Geography from the University of Portsmouth. During his time as a student he was a member of Southampton University Air Squadron and began his aviation career flying the Grob Tutor out of Boscombe Down in Wiltshire.

Donners joined the Royal Air Force and completed Initial Officer Training at the RAF College Cranwell in 2009.

Flt Lt Andy Donovan.

conversion course before being posted to C Flight of No. 27 Squadron. He has flown the Chinook Mk 4, 5 and 6A in the United States, Sweden, France and Germany in addition to multiple UK exercises. In late 2017 he deployed onto the strength of 1310 Flight in the Falkland Islands, under 905 Expeditionary Air Wing.

Andy is a qualified mountain leader and in his spare time enjoys travelling and spending time in the outdoors, cycling and playing squash. He is a keen photographer, specialising in military aviation imagery, and has also worked in graphic design and publishing. He will also be serving as the Deputy Display Manager for the 2018 season.

Weapons Systems Operator – Sergeant James Kennedy

Big K joined the RAF as a Movements Operator in May 2005 before transferring to become Non-Commissioned Aircrew in 2009. Upon completion of his Non-Commissioned Aircrew Initial Training Course and further generic role training, he was streamed to 'Rotary Wing' and posted to the Defence Helicopter Flying School to receive basic flying training on Squirrel and Griffin helicopters at RAF Shawbury. He received his Weapon Systems Operator brevet in 2011 and joined the Chinook Force, graduating from his conversion to type with No. 18(B) Squadron in 2013. K was subsequently posted to join A Flight of No. 27 Squadron, where he commenced his Combat Ready work-up.

He later worked at RAF Benson before being posted to the Defence Helicopter Flying School at RAF Shawbury in Shropshire, where he completed his basic and advanced courses on the Squirrel helicopters of No. 660 Squadron Army Air Corps and the Griffin helicopters of No. 60(R) Squadron respectively. After a short loan to the RAF Charitable Trust in support of the Royal International Air Tattoo at RAF Fairford, Donners arrived on the Chinook Force with No. 18(B) Squadron, where he completed his operational

Sergeant James Kennedy.

Weapons Systems Operator – Sergeant Gav Anderson

Ando grew up in Pocklington, East Yorkshire, and attended Woldgate College before joining the Royal Air Force as a direct entrant Weapons System Operator in 2009. After being streamed rotary he completed his multi-engine training course on No. 60(R) Squadron at RAF Shawbury and was subsequently posted to the Chinook Force.

During his time at RAF Odiham Ando has amassed nearly 1,000 hours on various marks of Chinook and has deployed

Exercises in Jordan, the USA, a detachment on Operation Herrick and numerous UK-based exercises allowed him to gain valuable flying experience, resulting in the award of his Combat Ready status in 2015. Since that time his role has seen him embark onto HMS *Ocean*, deploy numerous times to Norway and detach to the Falkland Islands. He was a member of the first crew to return Chinook operations to the Falklands after a ten-year hiatus in 2016 and now has in excess of 1,000 hours flight time on the aircraft.

Big K enjoys wine-making, horse racing and martial arts.

Sergeant Gav Anderson.

overseas with No. 27 Squadron to many areas of the world, including Afghanistan, Jordan, the United States of America, the Mediterranean and the Falkland Islands. Ando's most recent operational commitment took him to the Caribbean, where he contributed to the UK's provision of aid to the region in the wake of Hurricanes Irma and Maria, which caused extensive damage and left large swathes of the local population without their homes and livelihoods.

Ando sees himself as a Yorkshire man, living down south! An avid Leeds United fan, he enjoys attending matches in his spare time as well as getting out on his motorbike.

Sergeant Dave Cawood.

Weapons Systems Operator – Sergeant Dave Cawood

Dave comes from Cape Town in South Africa and moved to the UK in 2004, with the aim of joining the Royal Air Force. Dave graduated from the University of Staffordshire with a Bachelor of Engineering degree and was recruited by the RAF in 2008. Upon completion of his training he was posted to become a crewman on the Chinook. Since arriving on No. 27 Squadron, Dave has completed two tours in Afghanistan and flown on exercises in the United States of America, Jordan, Sweden and Norway. He has also embarked aboard HMS *Ocean* and operated from her deck in the Mediterranean.

Sgt Cawood has amassed over 1,500 hours on Chinooks and has recently qualified as a Crew-Served Weapons Instructor, which allows him to train more junior crew members on the operation of the M134 Miniguns and M60D machine gun, used to defend the Chinook on operations. He takes up this role alongside his other duties as a Maritime Unit Survival, Evasion, Resistance and Extraction Instructor.

During his free time Sgt Cawood enjoys watching Formula 1.

Display Team Manager – Master Aircrew Vince Bartlett

Vince was born in Cambridge in 1978, and he joined the RAF in January 2000 after completing his studies to A-Level. Following two years of training at the RAF College Cranwell and the

Master Aircrew Vince Bartlett.

With over 4,000 hours on type, MACR Bartlett is both a Crewman Trainer and Helicopter Tactics Instructor. As the Chinook Force Survival, Evasion, Resistance and Extraction Officer, he is responsible for generating training, procedures and equipment to develop the Force in this area and has experienced survival from the arctic conditions of Norway to the jungles of Belize and the deserts of Nevada. Taking a lead in development of future aircrew combat clothing and equipment, Vince was appointed as an MBE in the Queen's New Year's honours list in 2015. He is currently employed as the Senior Crewman on No. 27 Squadron C Flight, leading the flight's rear crew through training and development to ensure readiness for operations.

Vince is a keen drummer and enjoys many outdoor activities from skiing and hillwalking to climbing and kayaking.

Defence Helicopter Flying School, he gained his Air Loadmaster brevet and was posted to RAF Odiham and the mighty Chinook.

In his fourteen subsequent years of frontline service on No. 27 Squadron, Vince has operated in all environments from the Arctic Circle to the South Atlantic. He has supported operations and exercises globally, in the UK and Europe, Northern Ireland, the Falkland Islands, Norway, Sweden, Morocco, the Middle East and the USA. Vince has undertaken four operational tours in Iraq, eleven in Afghanistan and has previously been a member of the Chinook Display Team in 2009. Most recently he deployed to the Caribbean under Operation Ruman, contributing to the UK's support following the devastation caused by Hurricanes Irma and Maria.

Display Team Supervisor – Flt Lt Olley Leaming

Olley was born in Northern Ireland and educated in southern England before attending Sidney Sussex College, Cambridge, where he studied Aeronautical Engineering. He was commissioned into the Royal Air Force as a pilot in 2004 and was streamed to rotary wing. After briefly working in Joint Helicopter Command in a flight safety role, he completed his basic and advanced helicopter courses and was posted to the Search and Rescue Force in 2007, leading to him flying the iconic and venerable Sea King Mk 3.

Olley's first tour was on D Flight of No. 202 Squadron, based at RAF Lossiemouth, which saw him serve two tours

Flt Lt Olley Leaming.

training and Salisbury Plain Training Area, before upgrading to Combat Ready in March 2017. He later assumed command of B Flight and deployed onto the strength of 1310 Flight in the Falkland Islands as the Chinook Detachment Commander.

Olley is a keen hill-walker, skier and an enthusiastic gardener.

Engineering Team Lead – Chief Tech Marcus Ward

Chief Tech Ward was born and educated in Worcestershire and grew up in Bromsgrove, before joining the RAF in October 1990 at the age of eighteen, initially as a Propulsion Technician.

in the Falkland Islands detached to 1564 Flight in support of 905 Expeditionary Air Wing. He later transferred to No. 202 Squadron's A Flight, flying out of RAF Boulmer. In 2012 he completed the Qualified Helicopter Instructor course before being selected for promotion to Squadron Leader. He was posted to RAF Valley in 2013 before returning to the SAR Force to serve in a planning and air safety role during the transition of SAR capabilities from the Ministry of Defence to the Maritime and Coastguard Agency.

With the draw-down of the Sea King, he arrived on No. 27 Squadron in October 2016, where he initially fulfilled the role of second-in-command. During this time he completed detachments to Sweden, supporting European Helicopter Tactics Instructor

Chief Tech Marcus Ward.

His early service took him into the fast jet world, where he completed tours on Phantoms and Hawks, with an overseas posting to RAF Laarbruch in Germany, where he worked on the Visiting Aircraft Handling Squadron as part of the NATO cross-servicing team. Such duties saw him qualifying to re-fuel and support various aircraft types from across the alliance. In September 1997 he returned to RAF Cosford to undertake further training and upon completion was posted to RAF Coltishall in Norfolk and later Marham and Coningsby, where he saw the Eurofighter Typhoon into service.

As an Aircraft Technician (Mechanical), Marcus joined No. 27 Squadron in March 2015, on promotion to Chief Technician. He has undertaken many deployments from RAF Odiham, including to the Falkland Islands, where he oversaw the reintroduction of the Chinook after a ten-year absence. More recently he has been deployed on Operation Ruman, providing humanitarian relief to the people of the Caribbean following the damage caused by Hurricane Irma.

Chief Tech Ward is an avid fan of two-wheeled racing and regularly rides and restores motorcycles. He also likes to spend time sea fishing.

Engineering Team Lead – Sergeant Alan Brown

Sergeant Brown was born in Lancashire and grew up in Durham before moving to Norfolk. In 1998, at the age of twenty-four, he joined the Royal Air Force as a Propulsion Technician and since that time has become a Chinook man through and through.

Sergeant Alan Brown.

After his basic and then trade training Sgt Brown was posted to No. 18(B) Squadron at Odiham in 1999. He began working on first line aircraft maintenance with the Mk 2 and 2A Chinooks, where he built his experience of the type before going onto further training in late 2001. Successful completion of this saw him return to No. 18(B) Squadron as one of the last Junior Technician aircraft engineers and after four more years he was promoted to Corporal and posted to No. 7 Squadron. In 2014 he was selected for acting Sergeant rank and given the newly created role of Detachment Co-ordinator, which led to him taking responsibility for all engineering support aspects of deploying Chinooks around the world. By then falling under the banner of 'Aircraft Technician (Mechanical),' Al also acted as the trade manager and he also became involved in the introduction of the brand-new Chinook Mk 6 to UK service. On 1 January 2015 he was recognised for his efforts with a Commander Joint Helicopter Force Commendation. Promotion to Sergeant came in December 2015, which saw him posted to No. 27 Squadron to work in the manning and deployment cell.

His extraordinary eighteen years of service to RAF Odiham have seen him complete many exercises throughout the UK, as well as in Holland, Germany, Oman, the United States of America and embarked aboard HMS *Ocean* and HMS *Illustrious*. He has also completed several operational tours in Bosnia, Northern Ireland, Kuwait, Iraq and Afghanistan.

Al is an avid Sunderland fan and as well as regularly playing for his local town's veteran team, he is involved in coaching the local youth side.

2

DISPLAY WORK-UP

Preparations for the 2018 display season started way back in November 2017, shortly after the new team had been selected at RAF Odiham. Members of the 2018 team attended the Post-Season Symposium at the Defence Academy, Shrivenham, just outside of Swindon.

The UK display season typically runs from the beginning of May until mid-October and depending on where an air show is held, and who is responsible for holding it, UK aviation events can fall under one of two display authorities. Roughly speaking, anything that takes place at a General Aviation location falls under the Civil Aviation Authority (CAA) and any event at a military location falls under the control of the Military Aviation Authority (MAA). The CAA and MAA jointly hold two Display Symposiums a year, one in the spring and one in the autumn, and provide a forum for air show organisers, Flying Display Directors (FDDs) and all air show participants to get together to provide feedback on regulations, as well as discussing any lessons learnt during that season. By learning from the previous display season, the idea is that the next display season will be even better.

The 2018 team attended the Post-Season Symposium with members of the 2017 team to get an insight into what the season had been like, what had happened on the circuit and what lessons could be taken away in preparation for the following year.

The winter months provide the aviation community with a chance to recharge their batteries and while there are no air shows, the Chinook Display Team was already hard at work making plans for the RAF's centenary year.

The UK Chinook Force is a front-line helicopter unit controlled by Joint Helicopter Command (JHC) and is constantly on high readiness to be deployed anywhere around the world at short notice. In 2017 a number of aircraft were deployed to the Caribbean within a matter of days to assist with the Hurricane Irma relief effort, and just prior to the 2018 season starting, members of the team (and others) were scrambled overnight to assist the civilian authorities in Cumbria after heavy snowfall.

Some were also detached on a major UK tactics exercise at RAF Leeming until the week before the work-up period commenced.

Among the initial work to enable the display, the team were faced with a challenge that needed to be resolved before anything else could happen. 2018 would be the first year in which the HC6A variant of the aircraft was to be used and with this came some complications. The Chinook timeline is a complicated one but to keep it simple, the HC6A is effectively an upgrade of what were originally HC1 airframes in 1978 or HC2A airframes delivered in the 1990s.

The paperwork that is used to certify that a Chinook aircraft is approved for flight is known as its Release to Service, or simply RTS, and as the HC6A is ultimately an upgrade of an older model with the addition of a new digital automatic flight control system, this rather changed the playing field. From an engineering standpoint this was, in some respects, a new aircraft being put forward for display duties. Limitations that once applied to the HC1 in 1978 and carried through to HC2 and HC4 upgrades had to be analysed to re-validate things such as the rate of climb, maximum angles of bank or

Specially made platforms surround the Chinook while in maintenance so that engineers can access everything easily.

With the side hatch open, K checks the route on the in-flight navigation system.

pitch up and down. Work then needed to be done to prove continued validity of such limits on the HC6A or suggest amendment or removal in certain cases. With this work complete the HC6A was accepted for UK service but the impact on the display task, which operates the aircraft to the edge of its flight envelope, had to be fully digested to ensure that this more extreme mode of flying was still within the scope of the RTS.

Before anyone could get into the aircraft and start working up a display routine, Flt Lt Andy Smith, the Display Captain for 2017, needed to hand over the controls. The handover process started with lots of discussions on the ground and provided an opportunity for Flt Lt Smith to give an overview of how the previous season had gone, what challenges the team had faced and what sort of things to look out for at the numerous events up and down the country.

Display flying is considered the most difficult type of flying that any pilot can do as everything has to be technically precise and the routines are usually designed to show off the best of what that aircraft can do. Before Stu could jump in the

It was never a problem getting the main briefing room for the really early morning practice displays.

All crew have their own locker in the equipment store. The lockers usually contain essential clothing and gear tailored for each person.

right-hand seat and fly for himself, Flt Lt Smith flew several display practices to give the team some familiarity with what it was like to display the Chinook. The two pilots eventually swapped seats on 26 March and formal training for the 2018 display season was ready to get underway.

The Chinook display routine has remained relatively unchanged since the HC4 entered service and consists of numerous approved manoeuvres, so the only real difference year on year is how those manoeuvres link together. With the 2018 routine approved, Stu could take control in the cockpit, with Flt Lt Smith moving to the co-pilot's seat and one of the new display co-pilots in the central 'jump seat'.

Display practice sessions had to be scheduled in to the daily flying programme at RAF Odiham and the time slots were embargoed; this meant that all other flying on the airfield came to a stop to ensure that the team could practice in the full safety of knowing that the airspace was secured and entirely theirs for the duration of the session.

Display practices typically lasted about ninety minutes from the time that the aircraft started up to the time it landed at

The first set of practice displays were often flown with three pilots in the front: Stu in the right-hand seat, Andy or Schmitty in the centre 'jump seat' and Flt Lt Andy Smith in the co-pilot position.

Stu and Andy checked the outside of the aircraft together to ensure that neither of them had missed anything. The cable behind Stu is secured to the ground and is used to earth the aircraft when taking on fuel.

As the crew repositioned to run through the routine again, Vince discussed the display with the departing and arriving OC No. 27 Squadron.

the end. While the crew prepared to taxi and lift for practice, a team of people gathered on the edge of the dispersal and maintained communication with the crew throughout. This team typically consisted of Sqn Ldr Olley Leaming (Display Supervisor), Master Aircrew Vince Bartlett (Display Manager) and one of the RAF Odiham station photographers.

As Display Supervisor, Sqn Ldr Leaming would maintain communication with the team during practice, giving feedback on the display and ensuring that it was flown safely at all times.

During display practices Vince used radio equipment to communicate with the team once they were airborne. The radio communication would always be two-way to ensure that everyone involved knew what was going on.

Master Aircrew Bartlett was also responsible for communication and making sure that the team had everything they needed to fly a safe practice. The station photographers were responsible for filming all practice sessions so that everything could be fully debriefed afterwards using the video footage as a reference.

While Flt Lt Smith was in the process of handing over the display to the new team, the practice sessions were flown at 200 feet with individual manoeuvres flown independently of one another. Once each manoeuvre had been completed there would

be a slight pause in flying while Flt Lt Smith radioed down to the Display Supervisor and Manager with his take on what had happened. When all were happy, flying would resume and practice continued with the next planned manoeuvre. Once all individual elements had been flown and cleared at height, the crew would drop down to 100 feet and do the same again. This programme was repeated over a number of weeks before progressing into linking the display manoeuvres into thirds. Flying the individual elements of the routine independently was one thing but linking

The crew used to bring the aircraft into a hover to debrief on the sequence that had just been flown. This gave the team a chance to discuss things prior to moving out for the next run through.

The Chinook HC6A is also cleared to display with or without the side-door-mounted winch system.

them together in a way that looked smooth to those on the ground was another matter entirely. Practice displays quickly evolved and Flt Lt Smith soon stepped out of the aircraft; by mid-April the team were flying fully linked displays at 100 feet.

As was mentioned earlier, display practice times were embargoed at RAF Odiham. This was hugely important as the crew had to have no concerns about other air activity in the area as they built enough experience to be ready for their Public Display Approval (PDA). PDA for the Chinook Display Team is when Commander Joint Helicopter Command visits and decides whether he/she is content to approve the display in a public forum.

It's fair to say, however, that even when the display practices are booked well in advance, not everything always went to plan. Due to the operational commitments of the UK Chinook Force, things can change at a moment's notice and aircraft availability sometimes meant that the team could not get up for practice when they had originally planned to.

After a successful display practice and more than sixty minutes in the air, it was time to land and head inside for a full debrief.

The No. 27 Squadron C Flight office is adorned with some incredible artwork designed and painted by Andy. You may recognise this piece as it's a smaller version of what was applied to the No. 27 Sqn centenary aircraft.

The squadron's movements for the day were laid out on a big whiteboard with magnetic notes detailing crews, flight times, embargoes and aircraft availability. Along with a system that tracks similar information for the other squadrons at Odiham, this all came together to form a complex timetable that, for the most part, remained static. However, if an aircraft went unserviceable on start-up and the rectification work was expected to take hours rather than minutes, you could be mistaken for thinking that the whiteboard had turned into some sort of strategic board game as tiles began to move and the various 'players' started discussing priorities with the airframes that were left.

The key questions were asked – which flights, if any, could be shuffled around to free up an aircraft for practice? Even if an aircraft was identified, would it have enough hours left on the clock to be used for the display practice? Regular engineering checks are carried out after a set number of flying hours and more in-depth investigations are conducted post-display flights which again had an impact on other sorties looking to utilise the airframe afterwards. Further taxing the

Getting the correct weather information for displays was essential. Prior to the pre-practice brief one of the crew (Andy in this case) would check the Met Office data and insert it into the briefing pack.

Stu and Andy can be seen here collecting their equipment from the store room and signing the necessary paperwork before going flying.

The early morning sun was still rising as Andy took the essentials out to get the aircraft prepared for an early morning practice.

The Chinook HC6A is cleared to display with or without the nose-mounted Forward Looking Infrared (FLIR) camera. This can be seen just under the pitot tubes.

Above: All 'Remove Before Flight' tags are coloured red to make them easily distinguishable when walking around the aircraft. It is imperative that these are all removed before the APU is turned on.

Below: To the left of the Royal Air Force logo and mounted on the side of the aircraft, some of the Chinook's defensive aids can be seen.

Above: The canvas seats are dismantled and strapped up prior to display flying to give the crewman the maximum amount of room possible to move around in.

Below: With all the tags removed, Stu's final check was to make sure that the FLIR camera was secured properly prior to starting the APU.

Above: With all checks completed it was time to get everything prepared for flight.

Below: Looking out of the cockpit of the HC5, it's easy to forget just how beautiful the countryside looks from the sky.

Coming down from the first part of the rollercoaster in stunning weather at RAF Odiham. Affectionately known as 'Pegasus', this aircraft was borrowed from No. 18 (B) Squadron for practice.

planners was the requirement for the display airframe to be an HC6A.

The UK Chinook fleet consists of a mix of HC4, HC5, HC6 and HC6A aircraft, split between three squadrons at RAF Odiham and one at RAF Benson. Individual aircraft are also assigned to specific squadrons. It was therefore possible on a given day for No. 27 Squadron to have no more serviceable HC6As available if others were undergoing maintenance or if the display primary suffered an issue on start. At times a call to sister unit No. 18(B) Squadron occurred and the question was asked as to whether No. 27 could borrow an HC6A for the day, or for that sortie alone. No. 27 Squadron may have had plenty of serviceable HC5s or HC6s, but due to the different configurations the engineering foundation required across the various authorities in the UK would be immense to confirm that these were appropriate for display flying. There were (and always are) other far higher priority efforts ongoing which made this unrealistic. So, if No. 18(B) Squadron had an HC6A assigned to a flight but the tasking could use any type of Chinook, an aircraft swap could sometimes be arranged within a matter of hours, putting the team back in the air.

Early in the work-up programme, the display was not necessarily of the highest importance in comparison to other tasks but when PDA drew closer and Odiham had wall-to-wall sunshine, it was frustrating for the team to be stuck on the ground without an aircraft to practice in. Imagine going on holiday somewhere exotic only to get there and be told that you must stay inside for the duration of your trip; picture those levels of frustration and you're probably close to the feeling of being stood in front of that

While display practices were embargoed at RAF Odiham, the display had to occasionally land at short notice to wait for another flight to arrive or depart.

whiteboard at the time. Even when the display team did 'win' in such a scenario, it was likely at the cost of another training sortie that had taken hours to plan by another crew.

Unfortunately, this wasn't always a possibility and it was sometimes just a case of patiently waiting for the issues to be resolved by the engineering team. The engineering teams at RAF Odiham work around the clock to get the job done and without them it wouldn't be possible to maintain a capable Chinook Force.

Below: During practice displays the picnic bench was often carried over to a stretch of grass close to the disused runway. During the spring months a hot drink was essential to keeping warm!

Above: The two engines work together to drive both rotors on the Chinook. If one engine fails, flight can continue but in a more limited capacity. The rotors turn in opposite directions to generate the lift and are synchronised perfectly so that they never meet.

Above: The last manoeuvre of the routine saw Stu pull the nose up before departing to the hold.

Below: The Pegasus scheme seen here was designed by Andy and painted by the team at Serco. The scheme was put together for No. 28 Squadron's centenary and was the final of the three specials to be painted.

Andy also designed a badge/patch for C Flight. Coincidently, the wall art and PVC badge can be seen together here.

Engineers often work day and night to make sure that aircraft are serviceable and to meet the needs of the three front-line squadrons. Special hatches and doors allow access into even the deepest parts of the aircraft.

It's important to remember that while the display work-up training was going on the team still had their operational day-to-day job to work through. The crew had to maintain currency throughout the year and that meant that they had to undertake certain tasks, at certain times, to make sure that they were always in the best shape possible if they were ever to be called upon in an emergency. These taskings can sometimes be mundane but they are essential to keeping the UK Chinook Force in optimal condition.

Obviously with display duties, finding the time to complete these activities would sometimes prove to be problematic and often if the crew were to get out of sync, it would then have a further impact on their ability to carry out display practices at the times required. Scheduling time for these activities between practices at RAF Odiham became commonplace.

Maintenance on the rotor head required multiple engineers to work on different elements at the same time.

A spare part is carried up to the tail using the specially designed foot holes (hidden with spring loaded flaps) to climb up the side of the aircraft.

While work was being carried out on the two rotor heads, the blades were stored in a purpose-built stand in the centre of the hangar.

Above: Large green mats surround the aircraft while it is worked on. These mats provide a soft landing should anyone need it.

Below: The No. 28 Squadron special also featured a commemorative badge on the centre hook hatch.

Stu, Ando and Andy asked for a crew photograph to commemorate their first solo display practice, solo orange hand included!

Above: Stu and Vince caught up post-practice to discuss how they thought the first solo flight went.

Below: From the very start of the year the team were keen to get heavily involved on the social media platforms. An obligatory team selfie was uploaded to celebrate their first flight together as the 2018 display team.

Above: Ear protection is an absolute necessity on the flight line. The whine of the APU and constant thudding of the blades turning can quickly influence your hearing.

Below: It doesn't take long for the engines to warm up once the rotors start turning. Within just fifteen minutes the Chinook is ready to get airborne.

In the months leading up to PDA there was much more to think about than just the flying aspect of the display. The display team's season was to run from June, right on through to September, with just a small mid-season break in the middle. This meant that it was vital to get ahead of the game with as much logistical planning in advance as was possible.

If an air show wanted the Chinook Display Team to appear at their event, then they had to submit a formal request at the beginning of the year. These requests were sent to Joint Helicopter Command for review and then on to the team to see how feasible the event actually was; the decisions were usually based upon locations, dates, prior commitments and feedback on events from previous years. Back in May, the team received multiple requests for the season-closing weekend in September.

Throughout the display season the crew needed to maintain their flight currency and at times this was squeezed in between practice sessions. In this instance Andy needed to carry out some General Handling, so took to the far side of the airfield prior to running in for the practice slot.

The area at the rear of the airfield features a dummy deck of HMS *Ocean* (as can be seen here) and this allows the flight crews to train and get used to the space on deck.

The training area also features several different load options that the crews can lift when needed. The Joint Helicopter Support Squadron provides the hands on the ground when hooking is required.

One of the many skills in a Chinook pilot's catalogue is moving around on the rear two wheels. This can come in exceptionally handy when manoeuvring in a tight space. The crewman is essential in making sure that this is carried out safely and provides the much-needed rear-facing visibility.

Rough plans for the last weekend of the season came together with lots of doodling on the office white board.

The team knew that they were likely already committed to the Bournemouth Air Festival for at least part of the weekend, so they started investigating the possibility of also appearing at the Scottish International Airshow, perhaps on the Friday. Stu started sketching out some plans on the wall of the No. 27 Sqn C Flight office with some rough timings and crew information. It was known at the time that several of the crew would be potentially unavailable that weekend due to other deployments or personal commitments, so resource was already tight, and sadly after working it all out with transit times there and back, there just weren't enough available flying hours between the team to make it possible. The team always tried their absolute best to make as many shows as possible (within the number of displays permitted) but sometimes it just didn't work out.

As well as regular display practices and the logistical side of the air show season to keep the team busy, they also had several PR commitments to contend with in the run-up to PDA.

The first PR engagement was with Breitling and *The Gentleman's Journal* on a freezing cold March morning at RAF Odiham. The two companies were working together to produce a series of short films charting the RAF's first 100 years. Directed by David Gandy, the mini-series would highlight the importance of the Royal Air Force in today's global climate but also celebrate its vast history. The display team were selected as the voice for RAF Odiham and the Chinook Force, with the final film eventually being released in the July of 2018.

Always keen to get out and interact with as many people as possible, in mid-April the team were invited to the RAF Cosford Air Show launch event and this was the team's first real

The *Gentleman's Journal* captured a range of shots for their short film. The snow was already melting by the time the team got airborne.

Ready for the close-up? The hangar was filled with specialist recording equipment while David Gandy's team got to work.

With everyone on board, the ramp is retracted ready for the short taxi to the lift point.

Having landed at RAF Cosford, the team discuss the morning plans with the organisers of the RAF Cosford Air Show.

The team grab a quick drink before they're ushered out to talk to the waiting media.

Cosford was Stu's home show so the local BBC radio station was keen to get an in-depth interview recorded.

The first of many formal team shots that would be taken by members of the media over the course of the year.

exposure to the UK air show circuit. The event gave members of the media a chance to interview the team and, as a bonus, media personnel got the chance to go flying with the team to experience the mighty Chinook for themselves.

Shortly after the RAF Cosford Air Show launch day, the team was readying itself for the long transit flight to ILA Berlin: a trip that took several months of planning and involved an awful lot of moving pieces. Boeing was pitching the latest variant of the Chinook as a replacement for Germany's huge CH-53G heavy-lift helicopter, so the team

was invited to attend the air show and conduct several role demonstrations with a view to highlighting the Chinook's adaptable capability. The team had ambitious plans for the transit flight to the show and planned to stop at some of the major ex-RAF Germany airfields on the way through Europe; the team was even asked to help relocate an old English Electric Lightning airframe but sadly time didn't allow for the airlift to take place on that occasion.

With ILA Berlin out of the way, it was time for the team to re-focus its attention on the task at hand and to get in as much

Above: Dave and K took it in turns to give a guided tour of the aircraft and gave a brief overview of all things Chinook.

Below: On the way back from Cosford, a short detour was made to a nearby barracks to take on some fuel for the trip back to Odiham.

Ando checking into the Ops room to see what aircraft are serviceable and which cab the team has been assigned for the day's practice sessions.

There are usually multiple aircraft out on the pan first thing in the morning. This could be for sorties planned for that day or for engineering checks that require ground running.

The aircraft often required enough fuel to remain airborne for a maximum of ninety minutes during a display practice.

With his helmet on, Ando climbs up top to carry out some pre-flight checks.

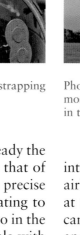

With the weather conditions pretty much perfect, Stu can be seen strapping in ready for the APU start.

Photography at RAF Odiham can be tricky as you can shoot into the sun for most of the day. During spring the sun moves around to the perfect position in the early evening and the light becomes ideal.

practice as possible. PDA was getting ever closer and already the display was looking like a completely different beast to that of just a month earlier. The flying looked punchier, more precise and much more agile than back in April. It was fascinating to see the evolution not only in the display sequence but also in the team itself; everyone was getting much more comfortable with each other and really learning to work as a single unit.

The restrictions and limitations put on the Chinook display meant that, if required, the team could still be practising later into the day and it wasn't uncommon to find the crew getting airborne past 18:00 for an hour of flying in the evening. Even at that time, you'd still find Olley sat out on the airfield in a camping chair giving the team as much feedback as possible and this feedback was crucial. From inside the cockpit Stu and the co-pilots had no idea what everything looked like from the outside until they reviewed the video footage in the debrief. What might have felt like a really smooth manoeuvre from

Above: Even though the cockpit has windows underneath the pedals, visibility of the ground directly beneath the aircraft isn't great. The crewman provides the eyes for landing and gives a talk-down as the Chinook comes to the ground.

Below: The countryside surrounding Odiham provided a stunning backdrop for the early evening rehearsals.

Above: The disused runway at RAF Odiham was used as the display line for all practice displays.

Below: After a long day of flying, the Chinook is taxied in as the last of the visible light fades away.

Being part of the display team always came second to carrying out everyday operations and sometimes this meant fitting in a display practice towards the end of the day, when most normal flying had concluded.

inside could have looked very sedate from the outside and likewise what the crew may have thought was an unpolished manoeuvre internally, externally would have looked fine. A lot of the feedback from Stu was to do with where he felt he could improve things but much of the time it wasn't too noticeable from where we were on the ground.

The end of April was in sight and while the team was almost ready for its Public Display Approval and the start of the air show season in May, there was some secret work going on behind the scenes at RAF Odiham. Andy was adamant to keep this from the team until the time was right; that time was PDA and it was just around the corner.

As the display work-up continued, the team invested in some more portable radio equipment ready for the start of the season. This enabled Olley to give feedback from the ground much more easily.

The underside of the Chinook features three hooks for heavy lifting; the central hook can take the most weight and sits behind a hatch when not in use.

3

PUBLIC DISPLAY APPROVAL

Public Display Approval (PDA) is something that every display team in the Royal Air Force must achieve before its displays can be performed in a public space. PDA is approved and awarded when the display and the associated team meet a list of predefined criteria and is the last challenge in the lead-up to the start of the air show season.

For the Chinook Display Team, PDA was booked well in advance of the start of training and it gave the team a point in time to aim for: Monday 14 May. The PDA process usually takes place behind closed doors and away from public view but for the first time ever, exclusive access was granted to capture the day in its entirety at RAF Odiham.

That Monday morning started like any other with an early morning briefing in one of the many rooms on the ground floor of the No. 27 Sqn building. Most Royal Air Force Squadron buildings (and bases to an extent) have a very similar layout. The ground floor of the No. 27 Sqn building has a large main briefing room at the far end of the long corridor with a series of smaller briefing rooms off the right hand side, and the operational and engineering offices to the left at the front of the building. Upstairs is an almost identical looking corridor but with offices either side and a squadron common room at the far end that's filled with history and memorabilia from No. 27's 100+ years of service.

With all mobile devices left outside in the corridor's pigeon holes (as is standard for all briefings), the crew took their seats in the large briefing room and the door was closed behind us, ready to start. Schmitty chaired the PDA briefing and started with the usual talk through of the display area and weather conditions, assisted by map data and the latest from the Met Office projected up on the large projector screen which adorned one of the four walls. The Met was forecasting bright blue skies and plenty of sunshine, but a slight on-crowd wind meant that the team would have to factor in a slight buffer in order to remain within the confines of the display box. Fortunately, this was a fairly common condition at RAF Odiham and the

Schmitty briefs the crew on the conditions for the PDA display while Vince and Olley cover off the formalities.

Only the two rear wheels provide the turning capability when on the ground as the front gear is static.

team was already very familiar with its requirements. Once Stu had finished his discussion on the display conditions, Ando went through the aircraft information. Unlike normal practice displays, the engineering team had prepared a back-up aircraft should the primary have an issue on start; at this point in the display work-up, and with so much riding on the outcome of the day, the team simply couldn't afford to not have a cab available for the day. Ando explained that the primary would be fuelled for up to an hour of flying and the secondary with a little less;

both cabs had more than enough flying hours remaining before their next engineering checks and the team was good to go. PDA is a very formal affair for the Royal Air Force and Olley was keen to emphasise that the team had to look its best ready for the afternoon's presentation; boots were polished to the max and all clothing was prepared to the very best condition possible and adhered to the strict RAF clothing guidelines. Olley also ran through timings for the day to give an outline of what would be happening, where and when.

As the briefing concluded, the team started preparing for their pre-PDA morning display practice: a final chance to polish anything that the team weren't already 100 per cent happy with in the air and an opportunity for Vince to run through the display commentary one last time. The commentary was something that had many iterations before the display season had even got underway. The script was based on that of the previous year but then torn apart and reworded with bits and pieces that were relevant to the team and more recent operations. Twelve

minutes may not seem like a long time to fill with dialogue but getting the timings right to coincide with the different parts of the routine was a real challenge to begin with.

While the PDA crew (Stu, Schmitty and Ando) were busy getting ready in the main building, Andy had a chance to shoot over the other side of the airfield to the Serco paint bay to check on a project that had been started much earlier in the year. Andy was responsible for designing the three epic pieces of tail art that adorned three Chinooks in recent years to celebrate

PDA is a formal affair in the Royal Air Force and there is a strict dress code for those involved. All flying crew were to be in their flight suits while senior members of the team were required to be in 'Blues'.

The team often relayed information to each other in between practice routines. Stu would give feedback on elements that he thought could be improved further while Vince and Andy could advise on how it looked from the ground.

Above: Climbing high into the highest point of the display; the opening nose over to crowd centre.

Below: Vince can be seen here running through his commentary, making sure that all elements of the script fit well with the display sequence.

The morning of PDA saw the team get airborne for one final practice and all aspects of the routine, including the commentary, were polished one last time.

As mentioned previously, the light at RAF Odiham can be a real problem, especially in the morning. Having said that, the weather couldn't have been any better for the team's PDA.

Earlier in the year Andy and James had to work out how the more intricate pieces of the design would actually be applied to the helmet.

the centenaries of No. 18 (B) Squadron, No. 27 Squadron and No. 28 Squadron over at RAF Benson. Just like the work on those three aircraft, Andy had once again teamed up with the guys and girls over at Serco to design some very special helmets for the team to use throughout the display season.

In previous years the display team have had several different designs applied to their display helmets (including a paint scheme reminiscent of the Jamaican bobsleigh from the Disney classic *Cool Runnings*) but nothing quite as ambitious as what

Andy had in mind. Working closely with James Littlejohn, the pair came up with a design that would not only celebrate the display team itself but also the RAF's centenary. As you'd expect, the design went through various iterations before they reached something that was both technically viable and financially feasible. The final design was incredibly complex and truly stood out as a piece of art in its own right; to say that Andy and James were over the moon with the finished helmet would be an understatement. What made this project so special

A number of different designs were sketched out and considered before settling on the final emblem for the back of the helmet.

Above: A whiteboard is used over in the paint shop to illustrate and keep track of the different re-sprays currently taking place.

Below: Layer upon layer of paint was applied to the helmets to ensure that they could take a knock without it having too much of an impact on the design.

Some of the more technical aspects of the design were applied using different vinyl colours. Much of the helmet work was carried out outside of working hours to make sure that it was completed in time.

James Littlejohn hands over the finished helmet to Andy after months of hard work from both of them.

was that it was mostly completed in their own time outside of working hours and, better still, the team had no idea that this project even existed.

On the morning of PDA the artwork on the helmets was just about completed but they were in no fit state to be worn. The helmets were completely stripped of parts earlier in the year before they were taken over to the paint shop, so they still needed to be rebuilt and fitted to each member of the team; each flight helmet is fitted to the owner's head and becomes part of that person's personal flight equipment. Andy's plan was to present a finished and complete helmet to the team upon achieving PDA but the hours were numbered. It was already 10:00 and there were less than four hours to go before it would need to be presented to the team. With the finished helmets wrapped in blankets and hidden away in the boot of the car, they were driven back over to No. 27 Squadron and secretly taken into the equipment workshop at the back of the vast hangar.

The equipment workshop was a hub of activity and was manned by a team of incredibly skilled workmen. The gentleman responsible for putting the helmets back together had been

Putting a helmet together takes a lot of skill and time. The average helmet can take up to five hours to piece together.

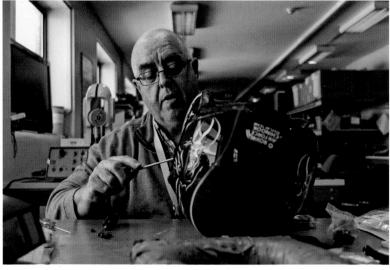

Patience is everything with a job like this. Constructing a helmet is much like putting an Airfix kit together.

doing the job for many years and would have been more than capable of reconstructing them with his eyes closed. The inside of the helmet was made up of a number of different leather pieces and padding, all sewn together in a particular way to ensure that the equipment stood the test of time. The helmets were taken apart at the beginning of the year when they went in for a service, so the first task was to find each pilot's bag of goodies. Each helmet would take up to five hours to put back together under normal circumstances so to get just one ready within three or four hours was a big ask.

Stu's helmet was laid out on the work bench, surrounded by small plastic bags full of all the different bits and pieces that were required to put his helmet back together. A number of parts appeared to be missing for some reason, parts most likely scavenged for a recent repair job, but that wasn't really an issue as the tall metal lockers on the far side of the room were well stocked with all the nuts and bolts you could possibly ever need.

While the helmet was being worked on in secrecy, the rest of the team were making last-minute preparations for the arrival of Rear Admiral Jonathon Pentreath, Commander Joint Helicopter Command. Joint Helicopter Command (JHC) was born out of the 1998 Strategic Defence Review (SDR) and saw the rotary assets of the British Army, Royal Navy and Royal Air Force fall under a single chain of command. Seeing as JHC covers all three services, the commanding two-star officer can be from the Army, Air Force or, in this case, the Navy.

The afternoon's proceedings started over at the main RAF Odiham briefing room located in the centre of the base. The spacious, slightly more modern, briefing room was the location

There was only enough time in the day to put one helmet back together; of course, it had to be the Captain's.

of choice for most 'visitor' activities on base and was a more than suitable place to conduct the PDA presentation. As Olley, Vince and Andy stepped inside, they were greeted by some familiar faces from Boeing. It was these guys that were responsible for analysing all the flight data recorded to make sure that everything remained within the aircraft's flight envelope. Commander JHC hadn't arrived yet but there was very much a feeling in the air that this was going to be an excellent afternoon for the display team. PDA day felt very much like a school on the morning of an OFSTED inspection: everything looked as good as it possibly could have done, and it was time for the team to show what it had put together over the last five months.

Group Captain Lee Turner, Station Commander RAF Odiham, led the Rear Admiral into the main briefing room to begin the afternoon and he was keen to instantly put everyone at ease by asking them all to relax and act like he wasn't anyone special. After a quick posed photo with the RAF Odiham guest book, Olley took to the front of the room, dimmed the lights and started running through the plan for the 2018 display season on the projector screen. The aim of the presentation was to convince Commander JHC that the team was in a position to fly at the start of the display season, which was just a few weeks away now. The number of practices and hours flown, along with the team's operational history, were fleshed out on the screen in front of everyone. The display sequence was discussed before Olley proceeded to a section covering the JHC-approved list of display appearances for 2018. A few of these shows presented some challenges due to the nature of the display boxes and the 'avoid' areas that surrounded the display box and it was at this point that Olley went into detail about what could be done to overcome those challenges.

PDA formalities started in the main briefing room with introductions and relaxed discussion.

While Olley was busy talking his way through the team's plans for the upcoming season, Vince slipped outside to get into position ready for his commentary. The team was already airborne and was out in the hold, getting sorted before the run-in to display. Earlier on in the morning Olley had traced the route that the PDA panel would take from the main briefing room out to the grassy area next to the disused runway with the aim of working out how long it took to walk from A to B. The answer to that very question was just under four minutes and the plan was for the group to arrive at crowd centre as Stu was pulling up into the nose over that started the display. Vince's other reason for being outside was that he was able to communicate with the guys while they were holding, letting them know whether things were running to time or not.

At approximately 14:55, the presentation wrapped up (bang on schedule) and everyone was ushered outside and directed to the right place. As the visiting group gathered on the wild patch of grass, Stu pulled up and was ready to start his display.

With Olley's presentation complete, it was time to head outside to review the 2018 Chinook Display and make sure that all the boxes could be ticked.

Vince ran through his commentary as if it were a public display while the PDA panel stayed quiet to take everything in.

The weather for PDA couldn't have been any better. Conditions were pretty much perfect.

Without knowing the display, it's tricky to understand how it all comes together and what will be performed next. Vince hands over a diagram to explain it all to Commander JHC.

What followed was an anxious twelve minutes as the team flew the display expertly through each manoeuvre. Conversation on the ground was kept to a minimum to hear Vince's run through of the display commentary but all eyes were on the guys in the sky. With the last pull away from the crowd, Stu re-positioned the aircraft into a hover just off to the side on the other side of the disused runway. Group Captain Turner and Read Admiral Pentreath briefly discussed the performance in hushed tones before turning around to Olley and Vince to ask if the team could run through it again. Why? Commander JHC was happy with the routine and was more than satisfied that it was all safe and ready for public display but felt that it didn't seem to have the right level of visual impact. A quick discussion took place and the team on the ground explained again that it was very much limited by the restrictions imposed (by Boeing) upon the aircraft during a display. Keen to see it again, the team was asked to fly the middle section of the routine as though it were

With the display seen and Commander JHC more than happy with both the routine and team itself, all that remained was for the formal paperwork to be signed.

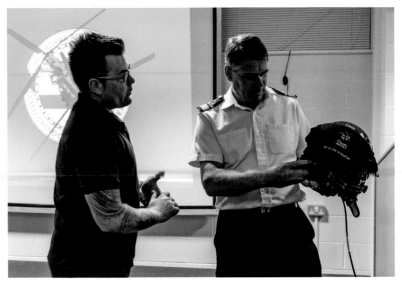

James brought the helmet over to present it to Stu and the rest of the team but Commander JHC took a keen interest in the design and the work that had gone into it.

over water and with the last pull away from crowd centre, the team was instructed to land.

As the group started the short walk back to the main briefing room, Andy disappeared back into the No. 27 Sqn hangar to go and grab Stu's helmet, which by this time was, amazingly, nearly all back together in one piece. While Andy was over in the kit room, the Rear Admiral took a seat at one of the large tables on the edge of the briefing room. On the table, neatly laid out in front of him, were the log books and related folders

for each member of the team and all that remained was for the formal PDA paperwork to be signed.

Stu, Ando and Schmitty entered the room to the news that they'd passed their PDA and had been approved for public display. While the team were busy talking through the PDA session with the Station Commander and Commander JHC, James Littlejohn stepped through the doorway holding the completed decorated helmet belonging to Stu and presented it to him in front of everyone. This was the first time that the rest

James talks Stu through the design and describes the sort of paint techniques that went into achieving such a high finish on the final piece.

of the team had laid eyes on the intricate design of the 2018 display helmet and the guys just couldn't get over the amount of work that had gone into it. Stu confessed that he thought Andy and James might have been up to something given the number of times that Andy had already had to disappear that day and, knowing the duo's history with special paint schemes, he was hopeful of something special.

The team was hugely grateful for all the work that had been put into the helmets and I think it's fair to say that for the rest of the year those helmets were treated like gold dust. Given the way that the guys handled them throughout the display season, you could have been mistaken for believing that they were the most precious thing in the world! Big K was first to get a nick on his helmet early in the display season thanks to his height and an accidental meeting with one of the fuel lines on board the aircraft.

With the formal part of PDA over and done with, it was time to make a clothing change for the rest of the afternoon on base. It's common practice in the RAF for a display team to wear a different-coloured flight suit to normal. Much like with the Red Arrows not getting their red flight suits until they've completed their PDA flight, all other RAF display teams get given their smart black flight suits on achieving PDA. These black flight suits were then worn at all public appearances throughout the display season, making members of the team easily distinguishable from visiting flight crews at air shows.

For the first time ever, the black suits were extended into the engineering team, making the 2018 Chinook Display Team an all-inclusive unit, and together they represented the very best of the UK Chinook Force up and down the country.

With PDA day drawing to a close, there was just one final thing to do: celebrate! The team made the short hop across base to the Officers' Mess for a sip of the finest champagne that Odiham had to offer, where they were joined by their colleagues for a celebratory drink.

PDA complete.

No celebration would be complete without a glass of champagne. The team were joined by colleagues after work to join in the celebrations.

After a long day, the PDA crew wanted one final shot in the setting sun outside the Officers' Mess.

4

THE DISPLAY SEASON

The 2018 display season was set to be one of the busiest on record with close to thirty displays over the course of just five months. The first show of the season for the team was the Duxford Air Festival in late May, just a couple of weeks after PDA.

The display slot was booked in for around 14:00 but the team wanted to be on the ground as early as possible in the morning to get the maximum amount of time in and among the spectators; this meant an early start in order to get airborne for 08:00. There was just one problem though: Odiham and most of the south of England was under a thick blanket of fog and, with very little wind, it wasn't going anywhere in a hurry.

The Met Office had the conditions flagged as red, easing to amber somewhere between 08:30 and 09:00, but one look out of the window confirmed that it was a somewhat over-confident assessment of the situation. The display and show had been briefed almost as soon as the team had arrived with a cup of coffee in hand.

Schmitty grabs his gear ready for the first show of the season.

K checks on the details of the aircraft that the team had been assigned for the Duxford Air Festival.

With thick fog covering Odiham, there was no way the guys were going to get airborne any time soon. Time to have a brew with *Friends*.

During the week RAF Odiham is a hive of activity with corridors and hangars bustling with movements. However, come the weekend it's more like a ghost town, with not a soul to be seen or heard in the squadron buildings unless there's an exercise going on.

With the conditions remaining static outside, the crew gathered in the Ops room to discuss the available options. As long as the weather at Odiham could clear enough to launch then in theory it would just be a case of getting above the fog for the flight up to Duxford. However, there were a number of things to consider. If they could launch but the weather deteriorated, where could

The fog still hadn't lifted so Stu talked through some of the different options that were available in order to get them to Duxford on time.

they divert into? The team couldn't get back into Odiham due to the lack of Instrument Landing Systems (ILS). Just a few days earlier the crew had to land in a nearby farmer's field due to the fog that was rolling in early in the evening; visibility had almost completely gone by the time the aircraft had touched down but fortunately the farmer was on hand with freshly made hot drinks to keep the crew warm. There were several different places that were highlighted as possible diversions but ultimately the decision was made to wait it out a little longer to see what happened. By staying on the ground at Odiham longer than was anticipated, the team missed the morning display briefing at Duxford, but this wasn't much of an issue as the Flying Display Director (FDD) was more than happy to give a one-to-one briefing when they arrived later in the day.

The fog eventually lifted enough for visibility to improve and with the aircraft fully loaded with everything needed for the day, the team departed Odiham and was on its way to Imperial War Museum Duxford. The flight was ever so slightly uncomfortable due to the persistent low cloud that stretched all the way from the south coast, right up to the Midlands, but as the team landed on the airfield, the weather was finally starting to clear. The forecast for the remainder of the day was blue sky and plenty of sunshine although I'm not sure anyone believed that at 07:00 that morning.

Before anyone had even stepped foot off the aircraft, the Chinook was well attended by the air show team on the ground and within half an hour the fire crew was being shown around the cab and being given a full brief on what to do if there was an incident at all during the day. While the fire crew

Orange hands at the ready and all the supplies needed for the day ahead.

There are many switches on the centre console and each and every one does something different. The collective can be seen to the right of this image.

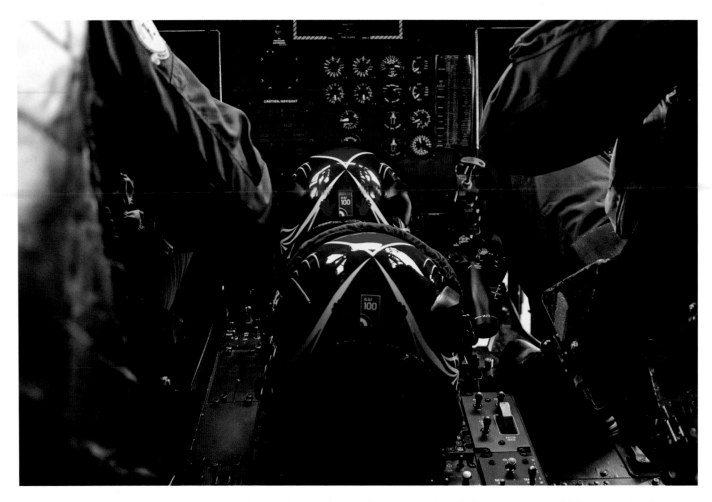

The team was finally able to get in the air and arrived at Duxford with no issues. These helmets were treated like royalty for the rest of the season as no one wanted to get any scratches or dents on them.

Vince shows the resident fire crew around the Chinook, pointing out emergency exits and detailing shut-down procedures.

The engineering team discusses fuel requirements with the Duxford team so that the aircraft is primed and ready to go later in the day.

members knew all of the airfield's procedures, this was the first time that they had been given such an in-depth briefing on the Chinook itself.

The engineering team was already busy refuelling the aircraft by the time that the VIPs arrived over at the cab for a guided tour and luckily tour guide Vince was on hand to tell them everything there was to know about the RAF's heavy-lift helicopter… and more if you had the time. With the show and tell out of the way and the aircraft handed over to the engineers, the team headed for lunch.

Andy wasn't flying the Duxford display and was instead in charge of social media on the ground. The team's use of social media throughout 2018 was revolutionary compared to previous years and that's thanks to the likes of Andy and Dave keeping it current and relevant across all channels while at shows. Social media has an instantaneous global reach, making it one of the best ways for a PR entity to communicate with its audience and most of the time it created a lot of interaction between the team, its followers and other display acts (both RAF and civilian) on the circuit.

All kit needed to be moved a fair distance from the aircraft, well outside the Chinook's rotor discs.

The truck was loaded up as much as possible before being driven to the staging point.

With nearly all the kit off the cab, Andy grabs a moment to update the team's social networks.

While Andy uploaded his shots, Vince was preparing for his first public commentary.

The crew was very well looked after by the Duxford team and after a hearty pie and mash in the aircrew tent, the minutes were ticking away, and it was time for Stu, Schmitty and K to head off to the aircraft and get ready. When preparing for a display, the team liked to head over to the aircraft with between sixty and ninety minutes to go; this allowed them to get 'in the zone', carry out all their pre-flight checks but also to relax a little just prior to starting the APU. Although Andy wasn't flying, he headed over to the aircraft shortly afterwards to join the engineers and observe the crew lifting for their

display slot. The rotors had been turning for about fifteen minutes and, with everyone well away from the aircraft, the wheels lifted off the ground and Stu took the aircraft out to the hold with ten minutes to go before he needed to run in to start the display.

Having taken a few shots of the departure to post online, Andy popped his gear back in the bag ready for the quick hop across the airfield to display centre where Vince was already hooked up to the speaker system, preparing for his commentary. There was a sense of anticipation in the air as this was going

The Chinook lifted about ten minutes before the display slot, just after the Wingwalkers had concluded their routine. Andy was able to grab a couple of shots while on the ground.

Mic checked and visual confirmed with Stu and the team: the 2018 display season was about to kick off in style.

to be the first time that the public would see the 2018 Chinook Display Team in action, and nobody wanted to disappoint.

Vince introduced himself over the airwaves as the distant sound of blade slap could be heard somewhere out towards the back of the airfield. The Chinook could never be described as a stealthy aircraft as it's famous 'wokka wokka' sound can be heard from over ten miles away and this was no different. The helicopter finally popped up from over the horizon and within seconds Stu was pulling the aircraft up into its first nose-over of the routine.

After more than three months of intense display work-up back at Odiham, the team was finally presenting the polished routine to the people on the ground at Duxford. As Stu brought the aircraft in to crowd centre for the final hover and pull up, the crowd roared into life to show its appreciation; the first display of the year couldn't have gone any better.

The display might have been over, but the day wasn't finished yet. The crew landed and had a short debrief on the aircraft before handing it back to the engineers for the post-display checks. Duxford was a day visit so there were only a couple of hours until the aircraft needed to be ready to get airborne again for the trip back to Odiham. While the aircraft was packed up and prepared for departure, the team members went their separate ways to spend a little time with family that had managed to make it to Duxford but before long everyone was back on board and strapping in ready to lift.

With everything in place, the Chinook was cleared to depart Duxford and moments later the aircraft was climbing to height for the transit back to base. Due to the thick fog and low cloud

The post-display team photo became a bit of a thing as the season went on. The engineers and flight crew had matching black suits for 2018.

earlier in the day, the trip to Duxford had been straight and level but that had all cleared now and the flight back was a little different. Given the beautiful clear blue skies, the team opted for a slightly longer trip back via the London heli lanes.

The heli lanes provide the quickest route from one side of the M25 to the other and on a day like that the city would look absolutely stunning in the late afternoon sunlight.

The aircraft approached the far east end of the city in no time at all and was soon over the Queen Elizabeth Olympic Park. The transit through London traced the path of the Thames and

With the display done, the team ventured into the public showground to meet and greet with some fans.

The flight back from Duxford took in the sights of London, starting with the Queen Elizabeth Olympic Park.

The London heli lanes trace the natural route of the River Thames.

swung by Canary Wharf, the O2, the Shard; the list goes on. Seeing the sights of London from the ground was one thing but to be above them and flying next to them was something else. Vince had fully lowered the ramp by the time the aircraft was over Tower Bridge and this gave Andy a chance to capture some shots of the city skyline for use on social media later in the day.

Stu brought the aircraft to a hover as we got to Vauxhall as he'd been asked to hold by Heathrow for some traffic to pass through. The air space in and around London is some of the busiest in all of Europe and NATS have the complex job of making sure that everything runs according to plan. With the surrounding area once again clear, Stu could continue with the flight out of London and, before you knew it, Odiham was in sight just a few more miles down the M3.

Having arrived on base at about 06:30 that morning, the crew finally climbed off the aircraft for the last time at 17:20 to be greeted by Ollie for a short debrief on the day. The guys were finally off base by 18:00. While those on the ground only see a

London has never looked so beautiful. Getting to see the city skyline from the ramp of a Chinook really was something special. This shot made its way into national newspapers just days later.

With the ramp down and the aircraft holding over Vauxhall, Andy jumped at the opportunity to capture a shot of Vince at work with the city in the background.

Buckingham Palace, Horse Guard's Parade and Westminster Abbey: London really is stunning from the air.

It's easy to forget just how much the aircraft moves when in the turn, as highlighted by the horizon in this shot.

twelve-minute display in the air, there's so much more that goes on behind the scenes to bring that display to a show, but finally, after nearly twelve hours on the go, the first show of the season had been completed.

The start of the 2018 display season was busy, with ten shows booked for the first eight weekends. After a quick trip down to Torbay Air Show for the Sunday of the weekend, the team quickly found itself at RAF Cosford just a few days later. The RAF Cosford Air Show was a complete sell out in 2018, with over 60,000 visitors in the ground. The show itself had a big focus on STEM (Science, Technology, Engineering and Mathematics) and RAF recruitment.

From the very start of the year the team members had decided that they wanted to focus heavily on public engagement as this was something that they felt had been slightly forgotten about in recent years. With such a big emphasis on STEM at Cosford, there was an entire hangar dedicated to showcasing the very latest industry technologies and providing a level of

It's not just the display teams that attend air shows. Colleagues from No. 18 Squadron were also in attendance at the RAF Cosford Air Show to man the mock-up Chinook.

The team took equipment to all shows that they were on the ground at so that 'kids' of all ages could try it on for size.

hands-on interaction that hadn't been seen at Cosford before. After a short stint in the Royal Air Force PR arena, the STEM hangar became a focus point for the team and the base for meet and greets that morning. The team was armed with stickers (designed by Andy) and posters to hand out to anyone that wanted them.

The informational booklet for 2018 was something completely new to the Chinook Display Team and a lot of thought went into getting it designed properly. With a little inspiration from their colleagues in red, the team utilised a folded booklet format that would open up into a large poster. While it would be the team handing out these poster booklets, the focus of the material itself was more on the UK Chinook Force in general. It was important for the team to stress that being display crew came second, always, to operational work.

It was another late afternoon display slot for the Chinook, which meant that the team members had plenty of time to continue their public engagement piece and explore the grounds of RAF Cosford. The team members couldn't walk more than twenty paces without being stopped by someone wanting a

The engineers were always on hand to discuss career prospects with the younger audience.

It wasn't just the aircrew that were tapped up for interviews during the season; the interest was in all aspects of the team and the guys were more than happy to discuss their jobs in great detail.

The Red Arrows couldn't get enough of the Chinook Display Team!

The team were asked to deliver a special message for the RAF centenary which was played across the BFBS radio network.

photo or for them to sign a poster; there had only been a couple of shows, but it was clear even at this early stage that the 2018 team was something special.

Cosford was Stu's home show; he grew up in Shropshire and was an Air Cadet when he was younger, like so many others that were working around the showground that day. After a chance meeting earlier in the day, the guys had been asked if they'd like to swing by one of the hospitality tents in the afternoon for a meet and greet with some of the lucky Air Cadets that were attending a VIP lunch accompanied by Air Commodore Dawn McCafferty CBE RAFR. Stu explained that dreams really can come true if you stick at it; he first attended RAF Cosford Air Show as a thirteen-year-old Air Cadet as part of No. 1119 Squadron and now nineteen years later was about to captain a display at that same show. Judging by the smiles on the cadets' faces, this was all the inspiration they needed to continue with their career in the Royal Air Force.

Above: Signing autographs at events became second nature to the team but they never quite fully mastered the art of carrying a pen each.

Below: It wasn't just members of the public that wanted their photo taken with the team; even those in the Royal Air Force (of all different ranks) were keen to get a snap!

Above: New members of the team for 2019? Only the very best dress in black.

Below: A treasured moment for the Air Cadets involved at RAF Cosford as they got to meet the team and hear how they progressed their career from starting out as cadets all those years ago.

The team managed to grab some time with the Chief of the Air Staff and discuss all things Chinook.

The engineers can be seen removing some of the tethers put in place to stop the blades moving when the aircraft is on the ground.

Despite being late in the day by the time that their slot came around, the air show was still packed out and most people had stuck around to witness the power of the Chinook helicopter.

Unfortunately, the same couldn't be said for the Sunday at Swansea. The Saturday had been wall-to-wall sunshine, but the forecast took a turn for the worse overnight and by midday on the Sunday, the cloud had rolled in and visibility had deteriorated. Another late afternoon display slot meant that the team had to wait around to find out what the weather was going to do. As the guys made the short trip from the seafront to Swansea Airport (where the aircraft was based for the weekend), the heavens opened, and it was looking like the afternoon flying programme may have to be cancelled before it had even got underway.

Stu, Schmitty and K arrived at the airport with plenty of time to spare. The engineers had been working on the aircraft and had managed to get the rain cover over the cockpit before it had started to rain heavily; while the Chinook is an incredible heavy-lift helicopter, unfortunately it's not the most watertight aircraft in the world. Andy and Vince had remained down

The crowds stuck around at the end of the day at RAF Cosford to witness the magic of the Chinook Display.

Ando can be seen in the side door as Stu climbs higher for the second part of the rollercoaster.

The RAF100 logo was applied to one of each type of aircraft in the RAF. Over the course of the season, this particular Chinook was affectionately nicknamed 'Stampy' as the decal looked like a postage stamp.

Just to prove that everyone in the UK Chinook Force loves their job! The engineers begin working on the aircraft as soon as the engines have been switched off. Keeping the aircraft clean of oil and dirt is a tricky job but quick work likes this goes a long way in making sure that it's mopped up as soon as possible.

Above: Stu, K and Schmitty spent some time on the beach at Swansea and spent a lot of time with the public prior to the display in the afternoon.

Below: It's not just the spectators that enjoy the Red Arrows. The team stopped everything they were doing to watch the full display at Swansea, the first and only time they were able to all summer long.

It's fair to say that the weather took a turn for the worse as the team headed up to Swansea Airport to get ready for their display slot.

The Chinook may be one of the most accomplished heavy-lift helicopters of all time but, like us, she still needs a rain jacket when it gets heavy!

on the seafront to stay close to flight control in case of any last-minute changes, and sure enough a change to the flying programme was made.

Stu received a call from Andy asking if there was any way that they could lift half an hour earlier than planned to get down to the seafront before another front rolled in. Luckily the aircraft was pretty much ready to go so just ten minutes later the team was strapped in and preparing to start the APU. By the time that Ando had got back down to the seafront from the airport, the heaviest of the rain seemed to have passed but unfortunately this meant that the crowds on the beach had all but disappeared. This was a massive shame, especially considering that the weather started to lift as soon as the guys got airborne from Swansea Airport.

A couple of days later and the team was back out again but this time it wasn't for an air show. In case you managed to somehow miss it, 2018 saw the Royal Air Force celebrate its first 100 years with several special events up and down the country.

Above: By this time in the afternoon it wasn't clear whether the display was going ahead or not. The weather up at the airport wasn't getting any better but word on the seafront was that the front was moving away.

Below: The aircraft has to be formally signed for and handed over from the engineers to the flight crew prior to display.

Sadly, the beach had pretty much emptied by the time the Chinook got airborne as the torrential downpour had driven a lot of people away.

The RAF100 setup at Horse Guard's Parade in London was quite the sight. Unlike many of the other 'aircraft' on show, the Chinook seen here was a real aircraft and was moved into London in the very early hours of the morning on the back of a low-loader.

Horse Guard's Parade is an incredible place and would be the location of the official RAF100 parade just a few days later.

As part of these celebrations, a Chinook was transported into London in the early hours of the morning long before any commuters hit the roads. The Chinook joined a number of other aircraft that had been put in position at Horse Guard's Parade as part of the RAF100 Aircraft Tour. The majority of the team was out in force to discuss everything Chinook-related and they were joined by a number of other people from RAF

Odiham to showcase the latest variant of the aircraft. July 2018 was one of the hottest on record and that Friday was no exception. Temperatures soared into the late twenties and early thirties. There's no doubt about it, Horse Guard's Parade felt like the middle of the desert, but luckily the Chinook was well acclimatised to those sorts of conditions. The exhibition was open to the public from 6 to 8 July and saw thousands of people visit over the course of the weekend, all helping to celebrate the RAF centenary.

Above: The display was opened to the public over the weekend prior to the RAF100 flypast and gave tourists a close-up of the RAF's past, present and future.

Below: The aircraft was kitted out to represent the operational side of the UK Chinook Force.

July really was non-stop. The team was down to conduct two different displays on the following Saturday: the first at Silverstone for the British Grand Prix and the second at RNAS Yeovilton International Air Day. This, however, all changed at short notice on Friday when the team's appearance at Silverstone was cancelled due to concerns over the risk of secondary crowds building up within the designated display box; decisions like this were not taken lightly and an awful lot of thought and consideration went into the decision before making the final call.

With Silverstone a no-go, the team only had to concentrate on Yeovilton. RNAS Yeovilton International Air Day is a large show and offered the team the opportunity to get in and among the crowd again. By this point in the season the team was getting quite accustomed to setting up a signing area for people to queue up and get autographs; the only thing missing this time was a pen! Luckily someone was on hand with a Sharpie and a signing disaster was quickly averted.

The sun was once again beating down on the south of England and temperatures were rising. Luckily the team had been sheltered in the hangar where they had been signing posters, but their session had now come to an end. Having spent the morning outside speaking with spectators, the crew headed over to the aircraft earlier than usual just to get some shade. As the aircraft was prepared for display by both the crew and engineers, tensions were running high. This wasn't due to anything related to what they were about to do: no, this was all thanks to England playing in the World Cup Quarter Finals!

Even though the referee was about to blow his whistle to start the game, the APU was about to be switched on and

By the time that RNAS Yeovilton International Air Day rolled around, the team had worked out that signing posters on a table was much easier than on someone's back!

all attention turned to the display once more. Stu and Andy had crewed in to the cockpit and started running through their start up procedures. K had also jumped on board and had plugged in down the back of the aircraft so that he could communicate with the pair up front. Checks were completed and the familiar whine of the APU kicked in. The rotors started turning and twenty minutes later the crew was up in the air for its display slot.

Above: Before the display, Andy familiarised himself with the display area once more. Preparation is everything when it comes to display flying; every location was different, and no two display boxes were the same.

Below: K straps the seats up ready for start-up and removes any loose artefacts from the aircraft.

While the crew wore white display t-shirts underneath their flight suits for most of the day, these were not allowed to be flown in. All crew had to change into fire-retardant clothing as a base layer to go flying.

Above: When the helmets went on and the headsets were plugged in, the crew no longer had to raise their voice over the noise of the engines and could return to normal levels of communication.

Below: Stu and Andy step through the engine start process together.

With the ramp down and the blades turning, K keeps an eye out the back for any potential FOD (Foreign Object Damage).

Above: The crewman is responsible for checking all angles of the aircraft to make sure that everything is running as it should be. The long cable and control in K's hand are used to allow communication with the cockpit while on the ground and in-flight.

Below: Stu runs in for the rollercoaster as the Red Arrows prepare for their departure.

The team was only six shows into the 2018 display season, but the routine was already looking much more polished than it had at the start. That's not to say that it didn't look good back in May, but everything was flowing cleaner and it was clear to see that the guys on board would not settle for anything less than perfection with each display.

It was now the middle of July and the team was approaching the mid-season break. Sunderland would mark the last show of the first half of the season, but before that the world's largest military air show lay waiting in the beautiful Cotswolds. It was time for the Royal International Air Tattoo.

For the aviation enthusiast, the Royal International Air Tattoo (affectionately known as RIAT) is the highlight of the display season and attracts visitors from all over the world. It is an event that acts not only as the biggest air show in the world but also as the single biggest social event on the aviation calendar. RIAT usually runs from the Wednesday of the chosen week to the following Monday. Wednesday and Thursday are

After a successful display at RNAS Yeovilton International Air Day, Stu and Andy bring the aircraft in so that the Commando Assault can get airborne.

K keeps an eye on the ground below as the freshly cut grass starts kicking up beneath the aircraft.

The downdraft from the Chinook's blades causes the grass to be swept up and then fall back to the ground like snow.

Display complete and time to grab some food as the Reds line up for their departure slot.

The team used the Media Centre as a hub for operations at RIAT. Dave spent some time talking to the Air Cadets about their future in the RAF.

normally set aside for aircraft arrivals and display rehearsals, Friday (at least for the past few years) is reserved for a small four-hour air display, Saturday and Sunday are the full eight-hour air displays, and Monday usually sees 99 per cent of the attending aircraft depart for their home bases and countries. Having said that, 2018 saw the addition of a full air display on the Friday to celebrate the RAF's centenary so everything was shifted by a day to account for it.

The full team was in attendance over the three-day weekend for the first and only time over the course of the display season. Due to RIAT being the biggest show of the season, everyone wanted to display at least once, and it was the only show where that would be physically possible.

The team headed to the Jeppeson Flight Centre each morning to grab a coffee and join the rest of the air show participants for the morning briefing. Each briefing lasted for about twenty minutes and outlined crucial information to the display teams; this ranged from safety information on display regulations, updates about the surrounding areas, in-depth weather updates from the Met Office and any notes from the previous day's flying. While the morning briefing was very much a formality, it was absolutely a necessity for all those displaying.

Above: Interview slots were booked in advance to make sure that the crew were available at the right times. Stu can be seen being interviewed for a local radio station.

Below: The entire team was on hand to sign posters for the cadets and passers-by.

Having attended the briefing on the Friday morning, the team decided to base out of the media centre for the day as this was fairly central to the showground and had good links to the internal road system in case they needed to get anywhere quickly. While the chalet was officially known as the 'Media Centre', over the course of the weekend it became more of a central hub for key goings on around the showground. A couple of interviews had been lined up with various team members for different broadcasters, so the team was busy for most of the morning, but it also gave the team a chance to relax a little and chat to people flowing in and out of the chalet. As the whole team was in attendance, this meant that everyone could conduct at least one display in front of their friends and families over the course of the three-day weekend; RIAT was the centrepiece of the display season and it meant an awful lot to everyone to be able to display in front of the sell-out crowds.

By mid-afternoon the team was in the air over the Cotswolds and in the hold waiting to run in. Vince had found his commentary position down at crowd centre in a large cordoned off area that was reserved for the media and those that needed to be in the commentary box. Given the glorious weather, Vince decided to take a seat at the table just outside the box; this gave him the best view possible as he could see right up and down the display line. The commentary box was more than adequate at most locations but more often than not the view was restricted due to the compact nature of the small room. For example, unless you could get yourself into a really low position close to the front window, you wouldn't have been able to see the Chinook at the top of the rollercoaster or nose-overs. Keeping visual contact with the aircraft throughout the routine was not

The Royal International Air Tattoo has a large area surrounding the commentary box and this allowed Vince to enjoy the sunshine and commentate on the display at the same time.

only important for safety reasons but also so that Vince could make sure that he was always at the right point in his notes. So much of the commentary referred to sections of the display that, had it been out of sync, it really would have been noticeable to those on the ground listening.

The commentary script had evolved a considerable amount by the time the team had arrived at RIAT. The commentary had started life in March as a crisp and clean sheet of A4 that was based on the previous year's display but by the middle of

The double-handed wave got an exceptionally warm reception at RIAT; it must have been like watching a huge Mexican wave from the air!

Positioning for the wingover at crowd centre.

the season it was more reminiscent of someone's revision notes with scribbles and highlighter pen all over it. While most of the commentary was delivered by Vince, there were certain times in the year where he wasn't available, so it was up to Andy, Schmitty or Ando to step in and take control. The adjustments were mainly around the delivery of the commentary rather than its content but even with minute changes it was interesting to see how much better it flowed compared to how it started.

RIAT isn't just a big show for the spectators, it's also a massive show for the aviation industry. Giants of the sector gathered at the show to demonstrate their latest innovations but also to host VIPs behind closed doors in their luxurious hospitality chalets. Most of these chalets served a three-course meal every afternoon to a select group of lucky people, complete with plenty of champagne! The RAF Chinook Force work extremely closely with Boeing, both in the US and at home in the UK, and the team developed a strong relationship with Boeing UK throughout the display season. The team was invited into the Boeing chalet on more than one occasion over the course of the weekend and this gave them a chance to interact with those responsible for all the hard work that goes on behind the scenes. Posters were signed and many a sticker was handed out, but it was clear to see that those responsible for the aircraft had an awful lot of interest in the display; after all, the RAF Chinook Display Team is the only dedicated platform for displaying the Chinook anywhere in the world.

Friday quickly became Saturday and before long the team was back over at the aircraft preparing for yet another display. Stu, Schmitty and Ando were on crew duties for the Saturday and were busy getting the aircraft ready for display. The engineers

The team had already met this aspiring pilot at Cosford earlier in the year and bumped into her again at RIAT; she was still convinced that the best pilots flew the Chinook.

had already done all the hard work, so it was just down to the guys to run through their final pre-flight checks. RIAT really is an incredible place and there is always something going on no matter where you look. As the team was carrying out its checks, the Battle of Britain Memorial Flight (BBMF) was conducting its display overhead in Trenchard formation; shortly after that the Lancaster returned with a Tornado GR4 on one wing and an F-35B Lighting II on the other. The GR4 came in for a final full-swept wing pass and thundered into the overhead just as

The team designed a limited-edition patch for RIAT and it was made in extremely small numbers. Patch swapping with other air arms is hugely popular at RIAT and you can often find air crew wandering around with patches on their arms that clearly aren't from their native display/air force.

Stu briefs Schmitty and Ando on the display conditions. It's not always possible for all members of the team to be at morning briefing so this quiet catch-up on the ramp was needed to get everyone up to speed.

This bear had already had a long trip by the time he stepped on board the Chinook. The bear and his logbook were taking a very special journey to raise money for charity and would be auctioned off at a later date.

Painting pebbles had become a bit of a craze with youngsters over the course of 2018 and this very special pebble was handed over to the team at RIAT. The aim was to get this RAF100 pebble as far around the globe as possible. One of the crewman was planning to take this to the desert in California later in the year.

The engineering team, complete with an elephant mascot (the emblem for No. 27 Squadron), watch Trenchard formation in the skies while taking a short breather from their work.

the Belgian A-109 shut down and the Ukrainian Su-27 spooled up just a stone's throw from where the cab was parked; where else could all of this happen in the space of just ten minutes in such close proximity?

The Su-27 starting up also meant that it was time for the rotors to start turning on the Chinook. All non-essential personnel stepped away from the aircraft and departed the live-side of the airfield and within twenty minutes Stu, Schmitty and Ando were taxiing out to the runway, ready to depart to the north-east to hold. While the guys ran through their final checks in the air, the Su-27 was being put through its paces in front of the Air Tattoo crowd; with the jet's wheels on the ground, Stu was already bringing the cab in for display.

The Saturday display at RIAT was by far the best display of the season at that point; from the ground it looked as though everything was nailed and the guys were more than happy with it once they'd debriefed back on the ground.

The weekend at RIAT gave the crew the first chance to try out the on-board GoPro camera systems inside the cab. The idea to get cameras installed on board was first discussed way back in

RIAT always offers up some exciting and unique opportunities. We were able to jump in the back of one of the 'follow me' cars and shoot the aircraft as the team taxied out for their departure.

The team were asked to hold briefly before flying out to the hold area. The Su-27 was behind them and would be displaying before Stu and the team.

April but the guys quickly realised that it was going to be a bit trickier than they first expected. The team wanted to mount four cameras in total: two in the cockpit and two in the back. Due to the vibrations on board, the cameras needed to be installed in secure mounts that wouldn't move around during flight and this meant that they would need to be attached to the inside of the aircraft in some way. As the cameras needed to be secured to the aircraft itself, the Release to Service would need to be investigated and the team ended up working closely with Boeing to get this updated so that the GoPro installation could be signed off. Getting something like this approved took a lot of time – several months in fact – but by the time the Royal International Air Tattoo rolled around, the cameras were ready to roll.

The team captured internal footage on the Friday which was then edited in the media centre throughout the Saturday morning, with an aim to get it pushed out on the social media channels by the end of the day. The footage showed something that up until this point had never been seen by those that weren't on board and gave a real insight into just what happened through various manoeuvres. The captured footage showed Dave completing the latter part of the sideways trawl, closing the ramp, stowing his big orange hands securely in the side netting and then moving to the front of the cab to the side door ready to be in a position for the climb itself; all of this took place in less than a minute and it was the first time that anyone had seen on-board footage like this. The months of work to get these cameras installed was well worth the result.

It wasn't just in the air that the team were kept busy though, as each day they also spent a lot of time on the ground.

The Sunday morning gave Stu, Andy and K a chance to try their hand at something a little different to flying. With very little encouragement and after a short chat with the RAF Bobsleigh team, all three of them were clambering into a two-man bobsleigh; to say it was a bit of a tight squeeze would probably be an understatement. Stu was in his element though and as a keen athlete was eager to also lay down on the skeleton bobsleigh. Stu was only a few minutes away from being signed up for the winter trials before they had to move on to their next location.

It's true that teamwork is everything when it comes to being in a display team but even the best teamwork wouldn't help three people squeeze into a two-man bobsleigh.

Sunday morning also had something very special in store. Outside of the RAF Andy had been a volunteer in the RIAT media team for a number of years and was all too aware of the sort of opportunities that could arise at short notice on the ground at the show. After receiving a secretive phone call from one of his friends in the media centre, the team was marched quickly down to the centre of the showground, where the RAF's

RIAT isn't just a big deal for enthusiasts and the visiting display teams, it's also a hive of activity for celebrities that have an interest in aviation. The team were incredibly lucky to spend some time with Sir David Jason on the Sunday of the Air Tattoo.

future training fleet was being shown off to the public. After a short wait Andy revealed to the guys that they'd be meeting and having photos with a legend of British television: the one and only Sir David Jason.

David Jason wasn't the only celebrity that they were going to meet over the course of Sunday either. The guys went their separate ways for the afternoon as a lot of them had friends and family on site that they wanted to spend some time with, but before Stu headed off, he met up with Flt Lt Jim Peterson, the RAF Typhoon Display Pilot for 2018. Typhoon and Chinook had built up a friendly rivalry since the beginning of the season and ended up spending a lot of time with each other at the various shows up and down the country. Stu and Jim had headed over to get some shots with some aviation products and ran into Carol Vorderman. Carol is also a keen aviator and flies regularly but has a much more important role with the RAF as the first female Honorary Ambassador for the Air Cadets. As if that wasn't enough, both displays were keen to get her seal of approval on social media!

The 2018 Royal International Air Tattoo was almost over, and the Chinook Display Team was one of the final acts to close the show in style. The early evening slot (just gone 6 p.m.) had the best of the day's weather with clear blue skies and a soft sunny glow. The temperature was still high, but everyone was in good spirits; RIAT had been a blast. Schmitty took to the commentary position this time around as Stu, Andy and K brought some of the loudest blade slap that would be heard all season long; the conditions were just about perfect.

Above: The weather at RIAT was sublime; not a cloud in the sky to be seen!

Below: Coming out of the central orbit towards the end of the display. This part of the routine was always a joy to watch as it allowed you to really picture the aircraft skimming the desert in an operational environment.

Below: Having knelt on the ramp myself more than once over the course of the display season, it is incredible that the crewman managed to stay so still for the duration of the sideways transit.

Above: The crewman can be seen clearly here at the side hatch. This position provided additional visibility of the crowd-line that the pair in the cockpit may not necessarily be able to see on their own.

In the turn and at power; this is when the beautiful blade slap could often be heard across the display venue.

The team had just over a week to recover from the intensity of five days on the ground at RAF Fairford before they needed to reposition to Sunderland for the two days of the show. Following on from Sunderland the team was due to make the trip over to Northern Ireland two weeks later for the Newcastle Festival of Flight but the team's appearance was cancelled by the event and as a result the next show wouldn't be until mid-August.

The seaside show down in Eastbourne has always been a favourite among display crews and enthusiasts alike.

In years gone by Beachy Head would have been littered with photographers, all wanting to catch the aircraft against the cliff tops and lighthouse as they held for their display slot. Sadly, with the changes to display regulations this was no longer possible and instead aircraft had to keep a much greater separation distance between themselves and the coastline. Eastbourne had lost a little of its charm, but it was still a big seaside event.

Like the shows at Torbay, Swansea and Sunderland, Eastbourne was an over-water display, which meant that the routing was flown at a greater height than those over land. Flying overland displays was a little easier than those over water. Over land you would have obvious reference points, maybe using a certain building or change in landscape as a point to aim a part of the display at. Over water this wasn't always the case as reference points such as buoys and boats would often shift slightly depending on the wind direction and speed. Not only that but the surface and texture of the water made it a lot more difficult to judge speed and altitude. A calm surface, for example, wouldn't give much perception of height as it just looked the same no matter where you were. Stu said that more often than not it really helped if the sea was a little rough and had some texture to it. Depending on the position of the sun as well would also sometimes create unwanted reflection on top of the water.

As if the everyday challenges of flying over water weren't enough, the first display at Eastbourne was conducted in less than ideal conditions. The engineers had moved down to Eastbourne by road on the Thursday morning as Schmitty needed to conduct his Instrument Rating Tests in a prolonged flight on the way down to Eastbourne. When required in certain circumstances, the crew must be able to fly using the instruments alone and keeping this skill updated was vital to everyday flying. The team flew through thick fog to get from Odiham to Shoreham, where they would be based for the weekend. The hope was that this weather would completely clear by the time the display slot came around, but the forecast wasn't getting much better. The Met Office had the cloud lifting and visibility improving just enough for the team to get airborne but judging by the conditions at Shoreham it would be very touch and go as to whether the team would be able to display or not. The team members decided to lift from Shoreham and make a call once they'd seen the conditions for themselves down on the seafront. It turned out that unlike at the airfield, the conditions down on the seafront had improved enough to display but the gusting wind certainly made for a tricky routine.

With Eastbourne completed on both the Thursday and Friday, the team moved to Biggin Hill on the Friday evening ready for the weekend's Festival of Flight. For those that knew the 2018 routine like the back of their hand, Biggin Hill was a slightly strange affair. Restrictions imposed on both the display box and surrounding areas meant that the team had to make a couple of changes to their standard routine. Earlier on in the year, as part of the conditions described in the PDA, the team was permitted to substitute certain manoeuvres for others should it be required; the rollercoaster could be substituted for either a single nose-over or straight and level fly-through while a wingover could be changed for a pedal turn. The Biggin Hill display box meant that the team was unable to carry out either

The team was located at the far end of the display line at Biggin Hill. Having taxied to the runway, the team was ready to get airborne. The angle at which the Chinook can take off will never cease to amaze.

the rollercoaster manoeuvre or the central orbits in the middle of the routine. This sadly left the display feeling like it was severely lacking something, but the team was happy to have been able to display in some capacity at such an important historic location.

The guys were also supposed to conduct a full display at nearby Headcorn on the Saturday for the Combined Ops show but the minimum height restrictions in the event permissions were not compatible with the Chinook display profile. The team never wanted to let any single event down and worked hard with the organisers to make sure that it could still make an appearance. Sadly, it wasn't the planned display appearance, but the team was still able to conduct a flypast and refuel on the ground at Headcorn, which ultimately meant that those on the ground still got to see the mighty Chinook helicopter in action.

The 2018 display season was coming to an end with just three shows to go; it had been an incredible year so far and no-one wanted it to end. A quick visit to Clacton Air Show mid-week reduced the remaining displays to just two: Dunsfold Wings and Wheels and the Bournemouth Air Festival.

Dunsfold was a familiar location to the team as the Chinook squadrons often conduct training at and around Dunsfold aerodrome. They obviously knew what the airfield and the surrounding area was like but had never actually flown a display there. Dunsfold is a fantastic venue for an air show; not only is it steeped in aviation history but it's also a beautiful location that's surrounded by wooded areas and rolling hills. We are now likely to be in the final years of any sort of flying at Dunsfold as the airfield has been approved for housing development and while the final decision is still facing a legal challenge, its future does not look good.

Stampy made her final appearance of the season at Biggin Hill.

Dunsfold Wings and Wheels is one of the most picturesque venues on the UK circuit and the rolling hills make for some beautiful shots.

Above: The clouds became quite dark at times but fortunately the displays managed to dodge any rain that was in the vicinity of Dunsfold.

Below: The crowd at Wings and Wheels grew steadily throughout the morning and by the time it came to the big orange hands, everyone was on their feet ready to wave back.

The bright green light on the underside of the Chinook is an anti-collision beacon. This helps aid visibility of aircraft from a distance during both day and night.

The original plan for Dunsfold was to fly there and back to Odiham both days but due to the amount of setup needed on the ground this plan changed last minute and instead the team stayed locally. This meant that the aircraft could be positioned down the far end of the airfield, close to the crowd, for all to see.

Everything that flies at Dunsfold just feels special: the action seems closer than anywhere else (even though it's no different to other air shows) thanks to the surrounding landscape and it seems the same is true for when you're in the air as the guys commented that it was perhaps one of their favourite display locations of the whole year. The smaller display box really lends itself to the tight routine of the Chinook and the blade slap bounced off the hangars over the far side of the airfield, echoing the sound right across the aerodrome.

With Dunsfold completed and the August bank holiday weekend now in the past, it was time for the team to prepare for the very last air show of the summer. The months had zoomed by and it was unbelievable to think that it would all be over in just three more displays. What made this even more surreal was that the team was preparing to fly out to California for desert training on the following Monday, less than twenty-four hours after completing the final display.

With the first photoshoot of the day completed, it was time for Andy and Stu to head to the kit room to get fitted for future deployments.

The team had been working on something very special for the RAF Odiham Families Day and a special planning meeting was required to make sure everything would come together at just the right time. The team planned to commemorate Boeing's achievements by conducting a flypast with *Sally-B*.

The RAF Odiham Families day also took place just a couple of days before the final show of the season and the team had been working on something very special. Following a conversation at Biggin Hill, the team was doing everything it possibly could to organise a unique flypast (and the first of its sort) to celebrate Boeing's incredible history: a formation fly through with B-17 *Sally-B*. It almost didn't happen, but everything finally fell into place and the families on the ground were treated to something that will quite possibly never be seen again.

Bournemouth traditionally has the biggest crowd of any show all summer long and 2018 was no different. More than a million people visited the Bournemouth Air Festival over the course of the four-day show and the beach was absolutely packed for most of the air display. The RAF Village at the

Above: A trip up to Air Traffic was required later in the day to make sure that the B-17 was still arriving at the scheduled time. Sure enough, *Sally-B* was local already and would be on the ground just fifteen minutes later.

Below: The flypast very nearly didn't happen due to some last-minute complications but thankfully everything fell into place and history was made with the first formation flypast by the two types.

Above: Families Day was a chance for the home team to demonstrate the Chinook's capabilities and No. 7 Squadron oversaw the large role demonstration.

Below: The Chinook can be used in several configurations depending on the requirement of the operation. A ladder can be seen attached to the central hatch, allowing for extraction.

Above: Fast-roping was also demonstrated. In the background you can also see two people connected to a line that's anchored to the rear door of the Chinook. This is another extraction technique not often demonstrated in public.

Below: The demonstration was carried out by a pair of Chinooks that worked together to complete the 'mission'.

far end of the beach gave the team the opportunity to give its new tent an airing. Most RAF display teams have a large tent that can be used for PR activities (you may have seen the Red Arrows tent, where people can usually queue up to get signed posters) but up until this year, the Chinook Display Team had nothing like it.

From the outset, the team was keen to make sure that it did everything it could to make 2018 an unforgettable display season and was adamant that it wanted to leave behind a legacy for the future. While the approval process took much longer than anticipated, by the end of the season the team had not only managed to secure a team vehicle for the foreseeable future but had also acquired a UK Chinook Force tent that allowed the team to set up on site and get a whole host of equipment out for people to interact with. The Chinook tent was an absolute hub of activity down in the RAF village and

The team had been working on a new strategic partnership with Jaguar Land Rover from very early in the year, but the team didn't actually get its new corporate vehicle until the tail end of the season. To celebrate the relationship, the team organised a special photoshoot with the new Land Rover Discovery and a veteran of the armed forces, the Land Rover Defender.

The team was keen to get some shots of the Chinook and Discovery on the ground together. In years gone by the team vehicle has been loaded on to the aircraft for such opportunities but the Discovery is a little too tall and can only get part way up the ramp.

A partial team shot with the Discovery was an absolute necessity.

The team had worked hard on getting a Chinook Force tent sorted for the display season, but one thing led to another and ultimately it wasn't available until very late in the year. That being said, it did manage to make it to a few shows and at Bournemouth it was a hub for all things Chinook and the public had the chance to learn a little more about the incredible people that work behind the scenes.

saw a continuous queue of people all day long wanting to meet and greet with those involved with the team. Some wanted to queue up and meet the pilots while others wanted to talk to the engineers to find out how they could one day also work in a similar job. The tent was manned all day, every day and the guys working down there were a credit to Odiham and the UK Chinook Force.

Bournemouth seafront was a glorious place for the team to end its season and while the crowd faced south straight into the sun for much of the day, the backdrop was more than worth it. The display box was marked at each end by the two piers and on 'Super Saturday' there were over 1,000 boats in the vicinity to watch the air show; this gave the team all the reference points it could ever ask for! As Stu brought the

Bournemouth was the very last show of the season. Just like that, the season had flown by at a ridiculous rate of knots. Bournemouth Air Festival has a dedicated media team that broadcasts live from around the seafront through the four days of the show and the team was keen to get a reflective word from the guys. Ando couldn't wait for his moment in the limelight!

Bournemouth provides the most spectacular backdrop of the entire season with the Isle of Wight to the far east of the display line.

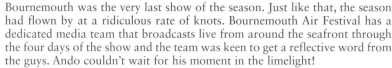

aircraft in for the final pull away from crowd centre, there were less than twenty seconds to go until the team could close off another chapter of its career in the Royal Air Force. The wheels touched down back at Bournemouth airport and that was it. It was done. For the Chinook Display Team, the 2018 display season was well and truly over.

Since the team members started flying their first ever practice sessions back in March, they had conducted nearly thirty individual displays over the course of five months. The 2018 display season had been a resounding success, and everyone involved was incredibly proud of what they'd managed to achieve. As the sun set on the horizon, the guys were already starting to focus on the next task at hand and before long they would be handing over the ropes to the class of 2019.

The widest part of the display allowed for the Needles to be brought fully into the composition.

Seaside shows are completely different to overland shows. Not only do they have greater separation distances, but they also allow for the full force of the Chinook's downdraft to be clearly seen in the water.

Above: Shooting south into the sun can be extremely tricky at times but there aren't that many places where you can get a Chinook and a Royal Navy vessel in the same shot!

Below: The final shot taken of the 2018 Chinook Display Team. It was an emotional sight, seeing the nose being raised for the last time both inside and outside the aircraft. 2018 was one hell of a special year!

5

BACK TO REALITY

Just days after the 2018 display season ended, the team was deployed to Naval Air Facility El Centro in California and Marine Corps Air Station Yuma in Arizona for Exercise Vortex Warrior and the Weapons and Tactics Instructor (WTI) Course respectively. RAF Odiham missed out on Vortex Warrior in 2017 due to other operational taskings, so the team was excited to get back out in the desert and train for future deployments. While those on the team were there to refamiliarise themselves and revalidate key skills like dust landings, new crews were also out there to qualify desert training for the first time.

Back in the days of the HC2, the difficult art of landing in a dust cloud was very much a manual skill and one that took an extreme amount of concentration and practice to get it spot on. Now however, with the Digital Automatic Flight Control System (DAFCS) in place on the newer models, this is a heavily automated procedure and pre-configured flight profiles allow the risk that existed before to be decreased by a substantial margin.

As with most desert environments, the increased heat certainly kept the engineering teams busy over the course of the deployment and while this may have led to longer than usual shifts to keep the required flying rate in place, it prepared them for similar environments in operational deployments to come.

Running alongside Vortex Warrior was the aforementioned Weapons and Tactics Instructor Course. Four Chinook Instructors and four students were provided to supplement fellow US Marine Corps delegates; this was the first time a non-US military service had been invited to take part in the exercise. After a long and strenuous classroom-based programme, the UK Chinooks flew alongside the incredible USMC CH-53E Super Stallions, and sometimes even accompanied by the odd CV-22 Osprey. The flying part of the course allowed the participating crews to fly several complex missions with the 'threat' level increasing as the scenarios played out, with simulated Man-Portable Air Defence Systems, surface-to-air missiles and heavy machine guns targeted at all assets.

Having been deployed for a considerable time since early September, it was almost as if the display season hadn't happened; within the blink of an eye, the summer had been laid to rest and it was back to the day job without a second thought. While it was a long and incredible year, it sadly couldn't last forever and by October the ropes were already being handed over to No. 18(B) Squadron for the 2019 season. That team will be quite possibly in the best position a Chinook Display Team has ever been in thanks to the exceptional foundations that were laid by the 2018 crew.

By May 2019, the new team from No. 18(B) Squadron will be heading for PDA and their display season will be just about to begin; they're in for one hell of a ride!

Members of the team trained out in California for Exercise Vortex Warrior. (Image copyright Joe Copalman)